REDUCING CHOLESTEROL

THE NO NONSENSE LIBRARY

NO NONSENSE HEALTH GUIDES

Women's Health and Fitness
A Diet for Lifetime Health
A Guide to Exercise and Fitness Equipment
How to Tone and Trim Your Trouble Spots
Stretch for Health
Unstress Your Life
Calories, Carbohydrates and Sodium
Permanent Weight Loss
All about Vitamins and Minerals
Your Emotional Health and Well-Being

NO NONSENSE FINANCIAL GUIDES

NO NONSENSE REAL ESTATE GUIDES

NO NONSENSE LEGAL GUIDES

NO NONSENSE CAREER GUIDES

NO NONSENSE SUCCESS GUIDES

NO NONSENSE COOKING GUIDES

NO NONSENSE WINE GUIDES

NO NONSENSE PARENTING GUIDES

NO NONSENSE STUDENT GUIDES

NO NONSENSE AUTOMOTIVE GUIDES

NO NONSENSE PHOTOGRAPHY GUIDES

NO NONSENSE GARDENING GUIDES

NO NONSENSE HEALTH GUIDE®

REDUCING CHOLESTEROL

A Heart-Smart Guide to Low-Fat Eating

with a contribution by Kenneth Cooper, M.D.

By the Editors of *PREVENTION*® Magazine

Longmeadow Press

Notice

This book is intended as a reference volume only, not as a medical manual or guide to self-treatment. It is not intended as a substitute for the medical advice of physicians. The reader should regularly consult a physician in general, and particularly for any symptoms. If you suspect that you have a medical problem, we urge you to seek competent medical help. Keep in mind that exercise and nutritional needs vary from person to person, depending on age, sex, health status and individual variations. The information here is intended to help you make informed decisions about your health, not as a substitute for any treatment that may have been prescribed by your doctor.

Library of Congress Cataloging-in-Publication Data

Reducing cholesterol.

    (No nonsense health guide)
      1. Low-cholesterol diet—Recipes.   2. Hypercholesteremia—Prevention—
    Popular works.
I. Prevention (Emmaus, Pa.)   II. Series.
RM237.75.R43   1989   615.8'54   88-26855
ISBN 0-681-40718-2 paperback

Compiled and edited by Marcia Holman and Jane Sherman

Book design by Acey Lee
Cover illustration by Jean Gardner

Photographs by Christopher Barone p. 16; Rodale Press Photography Department pp. 12, 28, 37; Christie C. Tito pp. 61, 76, 81, 87; Sally Shenk Ullman p. 44.

Printed in the United States of America

0 9 8 7 6 5 4 3 2

Contents

The Inside Story on Cholesterol

Human beings can't live without it, yet it may be partly responsible for one out of every two deaths in the United States. An essential body chemical, it is the building block of cell membranes, sex hormones, digestive tract bile acids and vitamin D. Yet, in excess, it can cut off blood supplies to the heart or brain.

It's cholesterol, and what you don't know about it can hurt you.

Although about 20 to 30 percent of the circulating cholesterol in the body comes from animal fat in the diet, the rest is manufactured by the liver. Americans eat about twice as much cholesterol as they need. Although the dietary glut signals the liver to produce less, it's a case of too little, too late. So the excess cholesterol, a white powder encased in buoyant capsules of fat and protein called lipoproteins, is carried through the bloodstream, where it clusters, like so much fish roe, in the walls of arteries.

The surplus cholesterol itself may damage the cells of the delicate inner lining of the artery. But the arteries may have already been left vulnerable by the pounding of high blood pressure or oxygen deprivation caused by cigarette smoking. In the presence of high cholesterol, and possibly as part of the repair process, smooth muscle cells filled with droplets of cholesterol proliferate and lay down a network of connective tissue in the artery wall. This becomes the basis of an arterial buildup called plaque. In time, this plaque can calcify, hardening like plaster.

But long before they turn an artery hard and brittle, these arterial plaques, part of a disease called atherosclerosis, clog a vessel the way fat and food scraps stop up a kitchen drain. Atherosclerosis, a progressive condition that may begin as early as infancy, can cause complications ranging from heart attack to stroke that usually don't appear until middle age. These complications account for one out of every two deaths and are the leading cause of permanent disability in the United States. Yet, in most cases, atherosclerosis can be lessened.

Although there may be a strong genetic factor in the development of atherosclerosis, it is in large part a life-style disease. It appears to be a plague of affluence, affecting mainly Western industrialized countries where animal-fat diets are the best that money can buy. And although the diet connection was long in coming, the scientific confirmation that diet contributed to atherosclerosis led many Americans to a new awareness with regard to diet. Many medical experts believe that the subsequent decline in Americans' consumption of cholesterol and saturated fats is directly connected to the drop in the death rate from coronary heart disease in the last two decades.

Reducing Cholesterol is aimed at helping you make some of the smart life-style changes that will help protect you from the unhealthful effects of excess cholesterol. It will show you how to have your cholesterol levels checked, what the numbers mean and how such measures as eating wisely and exercising can help keep your arteries flowing free and clear.

How to Check Out Your Cholesterol

How do I know if I have it?

If "it" is poison ivy, a broken leg or incontinence, that's a question you probably won't need to ask. At the very least, you'll know that something is very wrong—enough to propel you to the doctor, if necessary.

But heart disease is different. Too much cholesterol in your blood works insidiously over decades, depositing layers of plaque that narrow arteries, slowing blood flow to a trickle and ending in a heart attack that could be fatal. All this without so much as a hint of trouble beforehand, in many cases.

That's why having your cholesterol level checked is so important. It's like taking a peek inside your arteries, like a sneak preview that gives you the chance to avoid a bad movie. And you can. Doctors have found that reducing a high cholesterol level reduces the risk of heart attack.

So how do you go about checking out your cholesterol? The best place to start is at your doctor's office. The next time you're there, simply ask to have your cholesterol tested. Or call to make an appointment to have it done.

1

It's best to do it at a time in your life when your diet is not changing a lot and you're not gaining or losing weight—what's called a steady state. "People say, 'Oh, I'm gonna get my cholesterol measured' and start changing their diet to the way they think they should eat," says John W. Farquhar, M.D., director of the Stanford Center for Research

Cholesterol at Your Fingertips

There's a new technology afoot that could put cholesterol measurement at your fingertips.

It's called the finger-stick method, and its name describes the technique pretty well. A small lancet is used to prick a fingertip, and a drop of blood is all the machine needs to perform the test.

"The finger-stick procedure promises to revolutionize the whole area of detection of elevated blood cholesterol," says Michael White, associate director for prevention, education and control for the National Heart, Lung and Blood Institute. "It provides an almost instant analysis."

The machines will probably be in most doctors' offices and will give them the ability to take an analysis and counsel patients on the spot. "The way it is now, doctors lose a lot of time between when the test is taken and when the patient comes back in—if they can get them back in at all," says White.

But the machines can save money as well as time. It's estimated that a cholesterol measurement by the finger-stick method will cost under $5.

"Several of the machines have already been approved by the Food and Drug Administration," says White. "They're being used in some mass screenings, but we feel they still need to be evaluated and improved before they'll be considered a very reliable tool. There's a general optimism, though, that that will take place in the near future—within the next year or two."

in Disease Prevention at Stanford University. "It's better to see what it is on your usual diet, then if you want to experiment, you can change and see what happens."

The test consists of having a small tube of blood drawn from your arm—about 10 cc, or ⅓ ounce—not exactly the stuff horror films are made of. It's not usually painful, either. The blood can be drawn right in the doctor's office, although some physicians may send you to a laboratory to have it done.

If you're testing only for total cholesterol, the blood can be drawn on the spot. But if your doctor decides to test for triglycerides as well, you'll be instructed to fast before having the test. That means nothing to eat after dinner (about 6:00 P.M.) the night before the test. No chips during your favorite TV show. No ice cream during the 11 o'clock news. No real hardship. Schedule the test for first thing the following morning, and your fast will be over in short order.

Once the sample reaches the lab, a technician spins the tube of blood in a centrifuge to separate the cells from the serum. The cells end up in the bottom of the tube, with the serum on top, kind of like sediment resting at the bottom of a lake. A small sample of the serum is removed and a machine does the actual test. Depending on how busy the lab is, your doctor could have the results the next day.

What It All Means

The first thing to know about your cholesterol measurement is that you should take it with a grain of salt. "It's best not to think of it as a magical number that really is your number," says Dr. Farquhar. For one thing, your cholesterol level varies. "People know that there's variability in body weight, they know blood pressure bounces around and they need to be told that cholesterol bounces around, too."

There's also variability at the laboratory. "Some of the variation is technical. There are different methods for measuring total cholesterol that give slightly different results," says John C. LaRosa, M.D., director of the Lipid Research Clinic at George Washington University School of Medicine and Health Sciences, Washington, D.C. "And there's probably some variation within laboratories, too." For these reasons, and because there can be an occasional fluke, Dr. LaRosa recommends that you have at least two cholesterol measurements done within two weeks. Dr. Farquhar recommends having it done three times and taking the average.

What's a safe cholesterol level? A panel of experts met in 1984 to decide that question, among others. That "consensus development panel," set up by the National Institutes of Health, issued a chart listing the risks of various cholesterol levels in people of various ages. It's so detailed that it's a little unwieldy. But it's probably safe to generalize that a cholesterol measurement over 200 milligrams per deciliter may be cause for concern. "Ideally, it should be 180 or below," says Dr. Farquhar.

Another question you might have is whether to have your levels of triglycerides and HDL cholesterol (high-density lipoprotein—the protective kind) checked while you're at it. There's no definitive answer yet, but that aspect of cholesterol testing is being considered as part of the work of an expert panel on detection, evaluation and treatment of high blood cholesterol. In the meantime, most doctors recommend using total cholesterol as a screening test, then checking further if the level is elevated.

"You're not going to get agreement on whether all of the tests ought to be done on everyone," says Dr. LaRosa. "But there's reasonable agreement that a total cholesterol point somewhere around 200 ought to be a trigger for separating people who probably don't need any more attention (provided there is no family history of heart disease) from people who need a triglyceride and HDL test. If there is a family history of heart disease, you probably ought to measure triglycerides and HDL anyway." Some doctors measure triglycerides and/or HDL cholesterol as a matter of course.

Hold the HDL?

One argument for holding off on HDL testing is that it has even more problems with accuracy than the total cholesterol test. In addition, it adds considerable expense. While a measurement of total cholesterol averages about $25, a full "cardiovascular profile" may cost $60 or more. (Check with your insurer about coverage.)

If you do have your HDL tested, the lab can then also calculate the level of LDL cholesterol (low-density lipoprotein—the dangerous kind).

Basically, the more HDL, the better, and the less LDL, the better. An HDL below 40 or 50 is cause for concern; so is an LDL over 160.

But it's not cut and dried. Various genetic and environmental factors can influence these levels. Here's where the interpretation of the results gets pretty complicated—a good argument for doing all of this through your doctor.

Some doctors rely on the ratio between total cholesterol and HDL as an indication of risk. (The ratio is attained by dividing the total cholesterol number by the HDL number.) The lower the ratio, the better—that means that there's more HDL compared to LDL. A ratio below 3.5 would be considered ideal, and a ratio of 4.0 to 5.0 indicates about average risk. But there are situations in which the ratio method doesn't work. One of those situations is when the total cholesterol level is in the upper 200s. If a person has a total cholesterol of 280, for example, and an HDL of 80, his ratio would be 3.5, which sounds pretty good, right? "I'd still worry about that person," says Dr. LaRosa. "The HDL is high, but the LDL is also very high. I'm not too reassured by high HDL in the presence of high LDL." Dr. Farquhar agrees: "If the LDL is high, I want to see it down. I don't want to trust the protection of HDL."

The first step in lowering a high cholesterol level is a change in diet. "Regardless of your cholesterol level, you should change your diet toward the prudent diet," says Dr. Farquhar. "If the test indicates moderate or high risk, you should start pursuing it more vigorously."

Dr. LaRosa agrees. "Everybody should be tried on a diet first," he says. "Most doctors would agree that the American Heart Association (AHA) diet is appropriate. It's actually a series of diets that starts by lowering cholesterol and saturated fat content and increasingly lowering those components more and more as the 'phase' of the diet is increased." (Your local AHA can provide you with the details.)

Time to Change

Just don't expect immediate changes. "It takes time to get your mind made up, learn new habits of eating, change your palate preference around, get used to it, practice it and feel comfortable with it," says Dr. Farquhar. "Let's say that takes you two to three months. Once you've made the change, it takes only a week to ten days on that particular diet to affect your cholesterol level. Then you can go back and have your cholesterol checked two or three more times. If it hasn't gone down enough, then go into a more advanced nutritional-change program. Try that for three months. See if it works. If it still doesn't work, consider medications under your doctor's careful guidance."

If your doctor advises exercise and weight loss, you'll need even more patience. These can take even longer to accomplish than changing the nature of your diet. "After you reach the weight you think you'll be able to maintain, stay there for a couple of weeks and get into a steady state before you get your cholesterol done again," says Dr. Farquhar.

If your cholesterol level is normal, keeping track of it is a much simpler affair. "Assuming that your cholesterol level is normal, the AHA has somewhat arbitrarily decided on checking it once every five years," says Dr. LaRosa. "But that's assuming that there's no major change in health, weight, diet or exercise patterns." If you're very concerned, you may want to have it checked every year.

The age at which to begin testing is another subject of intense debate. "I think all adults should have a cholesterol measurement done," says Dr. LaRosa. "Whether or not to screen all children is still debatable. Children with a strong family history of coronary disease should be tested. And I think it's very practical to say that children who go to a pediatrician for any reason should have a cholesterol test. But most people agree that in children under the age of two, it's not worth being concerned about."

All about Triglycerides

Cholesterol always seems to get top billing when it comes to listing the fatty substances in blood that cause heart disease. And cholesterol has earned its bad name. But along with it on the computer printout of your blood analysis you'll see another reading, this one for trigylcerides.

We don't usually hear as much about triglycerides, perhaps because researchers are less certain about their role in heart disease.

One early analysis of data from the Framingham Heart Study, a long-term health survey of a Massachusetts town, found that by themselves triglycerides didn't seem to cause heart disease. But recently, with newer means of analysis, these same researchers have come to the opposite conclusion.

"New data show that trigylcerides *are* an independent risk factor for heart disease," says William Castelli, M.D., director of the Framingham study. "Anyone who has high blood lipids—cholesterol *or* triglycerides—should be considered a high-risk coronary patient."

Older women should be especially concerned about high triglyceride levels, according to these new findings. "Our recent data showed that high triglyceride levels are a terrible risk factor in women," Dr. Castelli says. "As a matter of fact, in women over age 50, it's a better predictor of coronary disease than LDL cholesterol. Believe it or not."

Doctors do use triglyceride levels as an indicator of health status. They agree that low levels are a sign of good health because they almost always occur along with low levels of other harmful fatty particles, like cholesterol. They also agree that high levels are at least indirectly associated with an increased risk of heart disease, because they are invariably accompanied by high levels of other harmful blood fats. In other words, triglycerides may do their harm independently, at least in some people. But they almost certainly cause trouble in league with other forms of fat in the blood.

Fat Energy, Fat Storage

Triglycerides are the biggest of the blood's oily particles. They are composed of three long strings of fatty acids attached to a sugar/alcohol molecule. Triglycerides make up almost all of the group of blood fats known as very-low-density lipoproteins (VLDLs), which is a large fraction of the low-density lipoproteins (LDLs), the blood fats known to cause the most harm to the circulatory system.

Triglycerides do two things. They provide the body's major source of energy from fat. Most of the fat and oil we eat is composed of triglyceride molecules. And they are the body's main storage form of energy. Much of the fat, sugar or carbohydrates we eat that we don't quickly burn as energy is transported to the liver, converted to triglycerides and moved back through the bloodstream to be stored in voluptuous thighs or rounded bellies.

Our bodies' fat stores are not static, although they might sometimes seem as fixed as the Rock of Gibraltar. The fat moves in and out of the bloodstream as stockpiled supplies are burned up and new stores move in. The more fat we have encasing our bodies, the more we also have circulating in our bloodstream. That's why Don Mannerberg, M.D., of the Nutritional Preventive Medicine Clinic, Richardson, Texas, former director of the Pritikin Longevity Center in California, calls high blood triglycerides "a kind of internal fatness."

"Just as we can get fat under the layers of our skin and in our bodies, we can have fat blood, so to speak," Dr. Mannerberg explains in his book, *Aerobic Nutrition.* That's also why most doctors agree that the best treatment for high triglycerides is losing weight, along with exercise and dietary changes.

The Greasy-Spoon Effect

Triglyceride levels in the blood vary greatly from hour to hour, depending on food intake. After a large greasy or sugary meal, levels can rise dramatically and stay high for hours. That's why a triglyceride blood test is always done after an overnight fast.

Normal triglyceride levels are based on age and sex. Today, most doctors agree that a "normal" range is from 85 up to 250 (milligrams per deciliter of blood). Mildly to moderately elevated levels, 250 to 500, pose double risk of heart disease in people with other risk factors. And severely high levels, 500 and above, are usually a genetic problem and can also increase the risk of heart disease if other risk factors are present.

Just how healthy "normal" triglyceride levels are is a matter of some debate. Because triglyceride levels do rise so much after a fatty meal, some doctors prefer to see lower fasting blood levels than those accepted by the American Heart Association (AHA).

"Studies have shown that trigylceride levels rise by as much as 120 points after a typical American meal of 40 percent fat and stay elevated for as long as nine hours," Dr. Mannerberg says. For people within the AHA's normal range, this could mean triglyceride levels rising as high as 300.

That has Dr. Mannerberg concerned, because studies have shown that as triglyceride levels rise above 200, red blood cells begin to clump together. This clumping blocks capillaries, decreasing oxygen delivery to the tissues, particularly to the brain. In its most severe form, it can contribute to strokes and heart attacks.

"Studies by Meyer Friedman, M.D. [who first defined the Type A personality], show that the ideal fasting blood level for triglycerides is 125 or less," Dr. Mannerberg says. "At that level, even if triglycerides rise after a fatty meal, they're not going to go high enough to cause clumping."

Some other doctors, though, including those on the National Institutes of Health (NIH) triglycerides panel, think there is an important difference between the "newly issued" triglyceride-rich particles that flood the blood after a high-calorie meal and "circulating" VLDL, which is present all the time, even during fasting.

They think the newly issued particles are less likely to cause coronary blockage because the molecules are whole, intact and unlikely to contain much cholesterol. The older circulating VLDL could be more harmful because it tends to contain bits of molecules that may more readily stick to artery walls. It also carries more cholesterol.

The Sugar Question

Perhaps the area of most dispute involves the effect of sugar on triglycerides. Some researchers think sugar is a major culprit in raising triglyceride levels. Others, notably a panel of blood-fats experts convened last year by the NIH and headed by researcher Scott Grundy, M.D., Ph.D., of the University of Texas Health Science Center in Dallas, do not consider refined sugar a significant problem except as it contributes to obesity.

"It is true that all sugars raise triglyceride levels somewhat and that refined sugars raise them a little bit more than complex sugars, such as starches," Dr. Grundy says. "But there is still some controversy about that. We're not absolutely sure." He thinks obesity, a high-fat diet and lack of exercise contribute to more heart disease than too much sugar.

Some physicians, though, put greater emphasis on sugar.

"I think it's fairly well accepted that in certain groups of people, even in amounts consumed in the typical American diet, sucrose- or fructose-containing carbohydrates will raise triglyceride levels, sometimes significantly," says Sheldon Reiser, Ph.D., head of the U.S. Department of Agriculture's Carbohydrate Nutrition Laboratory in Beltsville, Maryland.

Most likely to see this effect are people with noninsulin-dependent (type II) diabetes or a type of triglyceride-metabolizing problem. These people have high insulin levels when they eat sugar. They also have higher than normal levels of uric acid in their blood. For them, it's recommended that they avoid refined sugars, Dr. Reiser says.

But other people might also want to think about keeping their sugar intake low, Dr. Reiser says. "Sugar and fat work together to raise the fatty components of blood more than would either alone. It's a synergistic effect. The dangers of sugar are increased if you add fats, and the dangers of fats are increased if you add sugars."

Some people, especially those sensitive to sugar, also have high triglyceride levels when they drink and therefore should avoid alcohol, Dr. Mannerberg says.

Dr. Grundy agrees that alcohol can raise triglycerides "but maybe not in the dangerous way that obesity and diabetes do. People with very high levels, 500 or more, are prone to pancreatitis, a painful, sometimes fatal inflammation of the pancreas that is aggravated by alcohol intake. They need to avoid drinking."

Most people whose triglyceride levels are above 500 have a genetic inability to properly metabolize this fat, Dr. Grundy says. "There are actually two known conditions where very high triglycerides are found," he explains. In one type, the liver overproduces and pours triglycerides into the blood. This type apparently is associated with a high risk of heart attacks and pancreatitis.

In the other type, a normal amount of triglycerides is coming into the blood, but the body can't break it down normally, so blood levels remain high. "We don't think there is quite as much risk in this case," Dr. Grundy says.

But it takes complicated laboratory tests to determine which type you might have, and since in 80 percent of these cases it's a problem of overproduction, most doctors simply assume high triglycerides mean an increased risk for heart disease, according to Dr. Grundy. Any evaluation should include an assessment of other risk factors, including other blood fat levels and a family history of early heart attack. Treatment for these superhigh levels usually includes drugs to lower triglyceride levels and many of the diet and life-style changes mentioned below.

Treatment of Choice

What should you do if you're one of the millions of Americans whose triglycerides are moderately high, approaching 250 or more?

First, have three separate blood tests to confirm the diagnosis. "I do this to make sure the lab was correct and to establish a good baseline level before beginning treatment," Dr. Grundy says.

His treatment, in all but the most extremely elevated cases, begins with weight loss, exercise and dietary changes, not drugs. It's the same as both the NIH panel and the AHA recommendations, which Dr. Grundy helped establish. In most ways, it's the same sort of program you would follow to try to lower cholesterol levels and reduce most heart disease risks.

"I can't emphasize enough how important it is to lose weight," Dr Grundy says. "Even 10 pounds can help in people who are only 20 to 30 pounds overweight. Any extra energy the body has that it doesn't need turns into triglycerides. The loose calories floating around in your body that you don't burn up are made into triglycerides."

And that's why exercise is so effective, too. One study found that ten middle-aged men with triglycerides of 180 or higher were able to lower those levels an average of 25 percent by jogging, doing calisthenics or playing handball for one hour three times a week for four months. And they saw this effect even though their body weight remained constant.

There's no doubt that the typical American diet—high in saturated fat and cholesterol—dramatically enhances triglycerides' potential for harm. "You should make fat 35 percent or less of your calories to

This dish is more than an attractive menu item for a dinner party; it's also a heart-healthy meal. Fish such as mackerel, salmon and trout are an excellent source of omega-3 fatty acids, fats that may help lower triglyceride levels.

reduce this effect," Dr. Mannerberg says. In overweight patients, there's no need to replace this fat with other calories. For people within a desirable weight range, the AHA used to recommend replacement with polyunsaturated fats. Now, however, it recommends complex carbohydrates.

Dr. Mannerberg includes additional treatment for some patients who don't respond well to weight loss, exercise and a lower-fat diet. They cut out all alcohol and sugar and change their meal patterns so they don't gorge at night.

"I don't do everything with everybody," he says. "A lot depends on the triglyceride level, other medical problems and what the patient can tolerate. I prefer to put the main emphasis on life-style and diet, then, if we need to, add these other things as helpers."

He may have them eat fatty fish like salmon, or take fish-oil capsules. "There's good evidence that these oils lower triglyceride levels," he says. A study by doctors at the Oregon Health Sciences University found that triglyceride levels fell from 91 to 52 in people on diets rich in fish oils. These researchers concluded that the effect was due to the fish oils' ability to inhibit the synthesis of a protein used in the production of blood fats, called apoprotein B. The NIH panel on triglycerides suggests fish oils deserve a closer look.

"I think of life-style changes as the first and most important means of treatment of high triglycerides in most people," Dr. Grundy says. "And it's important to give these things time to work. I'd give them several months to a year before considering drugs."

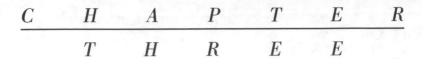
The Diet That Can Clear Your Arteries

"This is one of the greatest landmark studies in medical history."

"This new study and future studies like it will rock the medical profession on its heels."

"This research will forever change the way this terrible disease is viewed and treated around the world."

Thus spoke sober-minded scientists who probably couldn't have been more enthusiastic if they had been talking about a cure for cancer or AIDS. What they were beaming about was the first hard evidence of its kind to show something that many cardiologists say is impossible: *reversing* atherosclerosis. Not just preventing or stopping it, but actually undoing the damage.

Picture this: Like ice building up in plumbing on a cold day, cholesterol-laden lumps may be lining your arteries, slowly choking off the flow of blood. This, your doctor tells you, is atherosclerosis, or hardening of the arteries, the widespread symptom that's the main cause of heart disease. The lumps are lesions—ominous areas of blood vessel damage. And as they typically do in millions of people, the lesions grow relentlessly, nudging you slowly toward doom.

14

Then something odd happens, something almost unheard of: The lesions start to get smaller. Something puts the damage in reverse!

Evidence for this kind of reversal (or regression, as scientists call it) is precisely what all the fuss is about. Researchers say that in the new study, they used x-rays of blood vessels and strict scientific controls to demonstrate—better than in any previous research—that it's possible to make the artery-clogging lumps disappear.

What forced these dramatic changes in the arteries was the lowering of cholesterol in the blood through drugs and diet. And this news has sparked high hopes that diet alone may be able to literally clear your arteries—not just of cholesterol but also of the life-threatening roadblocks it helps cause.

In the milestone study, researchers from the University of Southern California School of Medicine tested and monitored 162 men with atherosclerosis who had previously undergone bypass surgery. The investigators first took angiograms (artery x-rays) of the men's diseased blood vessels to gauge the size of the damaged areas. Then they put half the men on a low-fat diet plus two cholesterol-lowering drugs and the other half on another low-fat diet plus a placebo (an inactive drug look-alike). Every patient's diet was monitored with a computerized analysis, and they did not smoke. After two years, the researchers took angiograms again of the same blood vessels and compared them with the earlier x-rays.

Contrary to conventional wisdom, the before-and-after angiograms showed clearly that dramatic changes had been wrought in the diseased arteries.

The researchers report that in over 16 percent of the drug-plus-diet group, the artery lesions got smaller. And, perhaps just as important, in 45 percent of this group, the lesions remained unchanged—meaning that the seemingly unstoppable march of atherosclerosis had been halted.

Even in the group on the low-fat diet without drugs there were encouraging signs: 36.6 percent had unchanged lesions, and 2.4 percent had lesions that shrank.

"This study demonstrates that we now have the wherewithal to turn heart disease around in its early stages," says David H. Blankenhorn, M.D., chief investigator of the study. "Years ago, scientists and physicians watched with satisfaction as a newfound treatment melted away

Researchers are finding evidence that reducing or eliminating such diet villains as high-fat junk foods may reverse damage already done to blood vessels. The American Heart Association recommends a healthy diet containing 30 percent or less of calories from fat and no more than 300 milligrams of cholesterol a day.

the early lesions of tuberculosis and stopped the spread of the disease in the lungs. And now we can watch again as a cholesterol-lowering treatment stops the spread of the lesions of atherosclerosis."

The Power of Diet

So just how potent were the low-fat diets alone in stalling or reversing artery damage?

"Unfortunately, our data can't tell us the relative importance of drugs and diet in affecting artery lesions," Dr. Blankenhorn says, "but clearly diet had an effect. We can, however, infer from our study that if people with atherosclerosis eat a low-fat, low-cholesterol diet (and don't smoke or have high blood pressure), at least 39 percent of them will have stable lesions—that is, their atherosclerosis damage will either diminish or stop progressing."

William Castelli, M.D., director of the renowned Framingham Heart Study, says that the case for the "regression diet" is very strong. "Dr. Blankenhorn's study and a lot of other research from around the world suggests that regression happens when you lower cholesterol in the blood—regardless of whether you do that with drugs or diet. So I think that in some people, diet alone can lower cholesterol enough to reverse the lesions of atherosclerosis."

That something as safe and simple as diet can reverse the seemingly irreversible still has to be scientifically confirmed, which very well could happen soon since there are at least 20 regression studies going on worldwide. In the meantime, we already have several clues to the possible makeup of a regression diet.

In Dr. Blankenhorn's study, the diet associated with the biggest impact on lesions (the drug-group diet) contains about half as much fat as the typical American diet. Twenty-two percent of its calories come from fat (10 percent as polyunsaturated, 5 percent as saturated fat and the rest as monounsaturated). And it limits cholesterol intake to less than 125 milligrams per day (about the amount in a roasted drumstick).

The diet responsible for the less dramatic but still impressive effect on lesions (placebo-group diet) is not as stringent—26 percent of total calories from fat (10 percent as polyunsaturated, 5 percent as saturated and the rest as monounsaturated), with less than 250 milligrams of cholesterol per day. This eating plan is only a step away from the even less demanding diets recommended to the general public by the American Heart Association and other authorities to cut the risk of heart disease: 30 percent of calories from fat and no more than 300 milligrams of cholesterol a day.

Most people can approximate all these diets by: (1) cutting back on servings of red meat, egg yolks, ice cream, cheese (except the low-fat kind) and whole milk; (2) making fruits and nuts the main source of desserts; and (3) increasing the intake of vegetables, whole grain foods, fruits and legumes.

Japanese scientists have also announced that with drugs and diet they were able to stop or reverse artery damage in 167 people. Reportedly, the diet contained very little fat and cholesterol—no animal fats, no cheeses, no butter, very little milk and no more than one egg daily.

In the Netherlands, investigators report that during a two-year period artery lesions in 18 people under treatment either remained unchanged or got smaller. The treatment: a vegetarian diet containing twice as much polyunsaturated fat as saturated fat and no more than 100 milligrams of cholesterol per day.

One Artery-Clearing Meal, Please

Here's a tale of three dinners. The first two menus are part of low-fat, low-cholesterol diets—like those associated with reversal of coronary artery disease. The third dinner reflects the typical American diet, which gets about 40 percent of its calories from fat.

18 Percent Calories from Fat

1 serving pasta with red clam sauce (low-sodium tomato products used)
1½ cups tossed salad (Romaine, lettuce, grated carrot, sliced cucumber, red cabbage)
2 tablespoons grated Parmesan cheese
1 tablespoon low-calorie Italian dressing
1 slice whole wheat bread
1 teaspoon soft tub margarine
1 cup coffee
1 tablespoon skim milk
1 strawberry fruit and juice bar
TOTAL CALORIES: 849
CHOLESTEROL: 45 milligrams

30 Percent Calories from Fat

3½ ounces baked chicken breast, skinless
1 serving brown rice pilaf
½ cup steamed carrots with dill

1½ cups tossed salad (Romaine, lettuce, sliced mushrooms, red cabbage, sliced cucumber)
1 tablespoon French dressing
1 whole wheat roll
1 teaspoon soft tub margarine
1 cup coffee
1 tablespoon 1% milk
1 baked apple
TOTAL CALORIES: 877
CHOLESTEROL: 93 milligrams

41 Percent Calories from Fat

1 cup onion soup
3½ ounces tenderloin steak, broiled
1 baked potato
1 tablespoon sour cream
½ cup green beans almandine, seasoned with butter and salt
lettuce wedge (⅙ head)
1 tablespoon Russian dressing
1 cup coffee
1 tablespoon half-and-half
1 piece pound cake
TOTAL CALORIES: 876
CHOLESTEROL: 181 milligrams

The Dietary Wild Cards

If these studies are any indication, a regression diet must contain far less fat and cholesterol than many people are used to. But if the aim is to reduce blood cholesterol enough to reverse artery damage, there may be ways to make such diets effective *and* easy to live with. Scientists are now investigating two nutritional factors that may lower blood cholesterol much better than anybody expected.

Water-soluble fiber.   A growing stack of research suggests that water-soluble dietary fiber—the kind abundant in oats, fruits, barley and beans—can dramatically affect cholesterol in your blood. It can lower total and LDL cholesterol (an extremely harmful kind) and raise HDL cholesterol (a beneficial type).

Right now scientists are particularly interested in a water-soluble fiber called guar gum, an additive in many foods.

"In studies we've conducted," says John Farquhar, M.D., director of Stanford University's Center for Research in Disease Prevention, "guar gum seems to significantly lower cholesterol, and other research institutions have had the same results. In fact, guar gum appears to lower cholesterol more substantially than fish oils or other dietary additives."

Monounsaturates.   Scientists have already shown that polyunsaturated fats (predominant in safflower, corn and other vegetable oils) lower cholesterol. They also assumed that monounsaturated fats (abundant in olive and peanut oil) didn't do much of anything to cholesterol. But now research suggests that monounsaturates may lower cholesterol as well as the polyunsaturates.

Niacin: New Promise from a B Vitamin

Still another approach to reducing cholesterol "borrows" from the world of nutrition. Studies have shown that when teamed up with a drug called colestipol and a diet low in cholesterol and dietary fat, the B vitamin niacin can help reduce cholesterol levels in people with hypercholesterolemia who have a genetic tendency toward superhigh blood cholesterol levels. Other research suggests that niacin can cut the incidence of heart attacks. Research like this suggests that niacin will someday prove effective as a part of any program for heart disease.

(You wouldn't want to try niacin therapy on your own, however. When used in this way, the dosages prescribed are much higher than the Recommended Dietary Allowance of 18 milligrams a day for an adult male, and you have to build up your tolerance to avoid side effects. So as a cholesterol-lowering agent, niacin must be used under medical supervision only.)

Regardless of whether anyone ever perfects a regression diet, the very fact that reversal of heart disease now seems possible will reverberate throughout the world for years.

"It's a marvelous instinct to want to have bad things like disease simply melt away," says one researcher. Now, at last, the instinct may come face-to-face with reality.

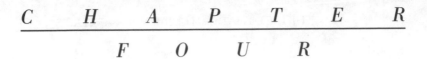

Using Dietary Fiber to Lower Cholesterol

Good health grows on trees! It hangs from apple-laden boughs and courses through crinkly spinach leaves. It hides in carrots beneath the soil and flows in waves of wheat.

And all of this good health is yours for the picking. Because every morsel of food that you get from plants—luscious fruits, crisp vegetables, flavorful grains—contains fiber. And fiber has remarkable power to preserve your health and prevent disease, researchers are finding.

You may find this fairly amazing for something often referred to as a nonnutrient. But the fact is, fiber is the term for the parts of plants that your body can't digest. In most cases, it passes right through your system. But don't be fooled into thinking that fiber doesn't have any effect while it's there.

The first step toward using the health power of fiber is knowing that there are actually several different kinds, each with its own unique ability to keep you well. There's cellulose (the most prevalent fiber, the one that made bran famous), hemicellulose and lignin, fibers found in whole grains, fruits, vegetables and beans. There's pectin, the fiber that puts the gel in jelly. And finally, gums, sticky fibers you eat without even realizing it. These plant-derived thickening agents are used in foods as different as bologna and ice cream.

One way to keep all of these straight is to think of them as falling into two categories: insoluble (those that do not dissolve in water) and soluble. The insoluble fibers—cellulose, most kinds of hemicellulose and lignin—are best known for their ability to ease constipation. The soluble fibers—pectin and gums—are making their name as cholesterol and diabetes fighters.

Lower Cholesterol
Means Lower Heart Disease Risk

If you knew that eating lots of delicious fruits and vegetables could lower your risk of heart disease substantially, would you indulge? If your answer is yes, you could be a double winner: You'll get to enjoy those fresh, sweet, juicy, crunchy foods that nature grows and probably lower your cholesterol in the bargain. Water-soluble fibers found abundantly in fruits and vegetables have been shown to lower cholesterol, and that can lower your chances of heart disease.

The fiber called pectin is an old-timer in the ranks of cholesterol fighters. As long ago as 1961, a study showed that eating pectin reduced blood cholesterol significantly. No less than 15 studies have confirmed those early results in the years since. Pectin has the much-sought-after ability to lower low-density lipoprotein (LDL) cholesterol, the undesirable kind, without touching high-density lipoprotein (HDL) cholesterol, the kind thought to be beneficial. What more could you ask?

You could ask that it have a greater effect in the people who need it most—those with extremely elevated cholesterol levels. It does. You could ask that it work together with cholesterol-lowering drugs to bring dangerous levels even lower. It does. You could ask that it work well enough so patients could take less of these drugs and avoid their unpleasant side effects. It does.

Studies have shown that a fiber called guar gum is equally as effective as pectin. And research at the U.S. Department of Agriculture is showing that other gums lower cholesterol, too.

In one study, Kay Behall, Ph.D., a research nutritionist, investigated the effects of three different gums—locust-bean gum, karaya gum

Quest for Fiber

Is there any fiber in what you're eating? If it's a plant food, yes. Fiber lurks in everything from vegetable soup to nuts. Check the table below for some representative amounts.

Food	Portion	Dietary Fiber (g.)
Vegetables		
Leek, cooked	1 med.	4.0
Kale, cooked	1 cup	3.9
Corn, cooked	½ cup	3.9
Brussels sprouts, cooked	½ cup	2.8
Tomato	1 med.	2.1
Carrot	1 med.	2.0
Broccoli	½ cup	1.6
Turnips, cooked, mashed	½ cup	1.5
Cauliflower	½ cup	1.3
Onions, cooked	½ cup	0.8
Green peppers	½ cup	0.8
Cabbage	½ cup	0.8
Spinach	½ cup	0.5
Celery	1 stalk	0.4
Fruit		
Raisins	½ cup	4.9
Pear	1 med.	4.5
Blackberries	½ cup	4.5
Prunes	5	4.0
Orange	1 med.	2.8

and carboxymethylcellulose—in 12 volunteers. Although they may sound strange, these gums are quite common. Used as thickeners or stabilizers, they are among the top ten ingredients (by bulk) in food production in this country.

The men ate muffins containing one of the gums (in addition to a regular diet) for four weeks. Then they switched to muffins containing

Food	Portion	Dietary Fiber (g.)
Banana	1 med.	2.7
Apricots	3	2.0
Peach	1 med.	2.0
Tangerine	1 med.	1.7
Strawberries	½ cup	1.6
Cantaloupe, cubed	1 cup	1.6
Grapes, seedless	½ cup	1.1
Grapefruit	½	1.1
Grains		
Oat bran, uncooked	1 cup	7.8
Oatmeal, uncooked	½ cup	3.1
Wheat bran	2 tbsp.	2.7
Whole wheat bread	1 slice	1.7
Rye bread	1 slice	1.4
Nuts and Legumes		
Kidney beans	½ cup	9.0
Pinto beans	½ cup	8.9
Split peas	½ cup	5.0
Peanuts	¼ cup	3.4
Brazil nuts	¼ cup	2.7

the other gums for four weeks each. For the sake of comparison, the men also spent four weeks on a diet with no added gum and four weeks on a diet with cellulose—a fiber known to have little effect on cholesterol —added instead.

The results were similar to those seen with pectin. Total cholesterol was lowered significantly in the weeks that the gums were eaten. Levels

(continued on page 28)

15 Ways to Eat More Fiber

How often do you eat the following?

- Several servings of whole grain breads, cereals, rice or pasta.
- Several servings of vegetables.
- Several servings of whole fruit, such as berries, apples and pears.
- Legumes, such as dried beans and peas.

The best answer for all of the above is "almost daily." "If you're doing that," says Sheldon Reiser, Ph.D., of the Beltsville Human Nutrition Center in Maryland, "you can't miss getting enough fiber."

But how much, exactly, in grams, do you need? It's a difficult question to answer. For one thing, there are different kinds of fiber. How can you give one number to cover a mixture of entirely different compounds? The optimum range is certainly going to be different for each one. And we don't yet know the optimum amount of each fiber. In addition, our methods of analysis haven't been perfected. That also makes it difficult to state exactly how much of each fiber is needed. Finally, people are different, and their fiber needs will probably vary, too.

The studies that have shown the benefits of a high-fiber diet seem to point to a recommendation of 20 to 35 grams per day of "total dietary fiber"—all kinds combined in sort of a lump figure. For practical purposes, a good guesstimate of the optimum amount is up to 30 grams per day.

The best strategy is to eat a wide variety of fiber-containing foods. That way you'll hit on all the different types of fiber and reap all of the benefits that fiber foods have to offer. And you shouldn't have to worry about getting too much fiber—the sheer bulk of the foods will keep you from overdoing it. Here are some hints.

1. When you think bread, think brown. Whole wheat (or other whole grain) bread should be the rule, not the exception.
2. Satisfy your sweet tooth with fruit. Berries, apples, bananas and peaches make excellent desserts.
3. Look for salad bars that offer a wide variety of fresh vegetables—not just lettuce. And make that kind of salad at home.
4. Eat high-fiber cereals regularly for breakfast.
5. Don't peel apples, pears or peaches when you bake them.
6. Eat potatoes and other vegetables with their skins.
7. Eat vegetables that have edible stems or stalks, such as broccoli.
8. Eat fruits that have edible seeds, such as raspberries, blackberries and strawberries.
9. Eat dried fruits, such as apricots, prunes and raisins. Fiber is more concentrated in them (but so are the calories).
10. Eat the membranes that cling to oranges and grapefruit when you peel them.
11. Snack on seeds.
12. Substitute beans for beef in chili or casseroles.
13. Munch on popcorn.
14. Add barley to vegetable soups.
15. Remember that whole grain doesn't have to mean bread or cereal. Try brown rice, corn tortillas, bulgur wheat or whole wheat pasta.

dropped from an average of 200 (not very high to begin with) to 170. And as with pectin, HDL cholesterol was unaffected. Cholesterol did not drop during the weeks the men ate cellulose or no added fiber.

In other studies, people with extremely high cholesterol levels saw those levels reduced after eating foods that included a granolalike bar with either guar or locust-bean gum added. They were also able to reduce the amount of cholesterol-lowering drugs they were taking.

While wheat bran doesn't seem to have much effect on cholesterol (it's mostly cellulose), oat bran, with its large proportion of water-soluble gum, can reduce cholesterol levels dramatically. Corn bran falls somewhere in the middle.

What do all of these water-soluble fibers have in common, and how do they lower cholesterol? The most important thing seems to be the ability to form a gel with water in the intestines.

Normally, digestive substances called bile acids are secreted into the small intestine following a meal. After they do their job, they're reabsorbed. These bile acids are made from cholesterol. "The feeling is that when you eat water-soluble fibers, such as pectin or gums, bile acids become entrapped in the gel and are carried into the large in-

Oranges, besides being delicious, refreshing and high in vitamin C, contain significant amounts of pectin, a type of soluble fiber that has been shown to reduce blood levels of cholesterol.

testine, where they can no longer be reabsorbed," explains Dr. Behall. "The body then has to take cholesterol out of the blood to produce more bile acids. In addition, some of the cholesterol you eat may get caught up in the gel and be excreted from the body, too."

Oat bran and dried beans are the only good food sources of gum that you can buy at the supermarket right now. The other gums are available only on a commercial basis. Dr. Behall believes that someday they will also be available in the supermarket, baked into granola bars or muffins made specifically for people with elevated cholesterol levels or diabetes.

But pectin is readily available—in fruits and vegetables. Studies show that the amount necessary to lower cholesterol is eight to ten grams a day—the amount in four oranges, for example.

Ease into Eating Fiber

If you're ready to give fiber a try, you may want to take it easy on your system and get started in a gradual way, because it takes a little while for your innards to adapt to a high-fiber diet. Otherwise, you might feel a little uncomfortable ("What's all this rumbling and grumbling in my gut?"), and you don't want to be discouraged right off the bat. So try phasing it in over a week or more, until you find a level that's comfortable for you. And here's another tip: If you add bran to your diet, drink more water to keep things humming along. (One overly enthusiastic gentleman started off his fiber program by eating two *cups* of bran at a sitting, with very little milk. As a result, he had to have a plug of fiber surgically removed from his intestine. The moral of the story: Don't go overboard.)

Activated Charcoal: New Champion of Cholesterol Fighters?

Charcoal is catching fire.

Not just any charcoal, and certainly not what you use to grill your chicken and fill the neighbor's backyard with smoke.

It's activated charcoal — wood, nutshells or vegetable matter that is roasted without oxygen until it is glossy black, then ground into fine particles and steamed at very high temperatures to open the pinpoint pores dotting each particle's surface.

Because these pores have been found to latch onto certain fluids and gases, activated charcoal is a natural, all-purpose filter. You'll find it in foot pads to snuff out sneaker odor, for instance. But in a purified form it is also used as an oral antidote for people who've swallowed poison or overdosed on drugs. It can also be taken to control uncomfortable intestinal gas.

Now activated charcoal is being auditioned for a new and potentially heart-saving role: lowering cholesterol. Early results suggest it might be more powerful than conventional drug treatment, with none of the side effects.

A study by scientists in Finland has made charcoal a hot topic among researchers in the United States.

Seven patients in the Finnish study were given about ¼ ounce of activated charcoal three times a day for four weeks. At the end, their blood levels of low-density lipoprotein (LDL) cholesterol—the harmful kind that clogs arteries—had fallen 41 percent. To put these results in perspective, consider that conventional drugs lower LDL by only about 16 percent.

At the same time, levels of high-density lipoprotein (HDL) cholesterol rose slightly. HDL is considered a protective factor against heart disease.

Although raising HDL is beneficial, it's also important to reduce cholesterol levels overall. High levels of total cholesterol have been linked with increased risk of heart disease.

Charcoal's Magnetic Personality

To Eli A. Friedman, M.D., a medical researcher at the State University of New York Health Science Center in Brooklyn, these findings strongly indicate a need to investigate activated charcoal further.

"The key question is its efficiency," he says. "Will it work in more than seven people?"

On the basis of the Finnish study and previous research of his own, Dr. Friedman suspects charcoal may lower cholesterol by binding, or clinging to it. Here's how it works.

Picture the surface of a grain of activated charcoal as something like the face of a microscopic moon, with craters of many sizes, from small to large. Scientists have long known that molecules of certain substances —intestinal gas or poison, for example—are attracted to these holes.

When molecules want to move in, a bit of charcoal can be very accommodating. Because each grain has pores of many different sizes and shapes, it gives molecules of varying sizes and shapes places to roost. A hefty molecule of cholesterol might slip into one cranny, while a much smaller molecule of intestinal gas would fit into another.

One of the advantages of activated charcoal is that the body doesn't absorb it from the intestine. Charcoal simply picks up molecules, like passengers on a bus, and heads for the nearest exit ramp out of the body. That's what makes charcoal so safe.

If charcoal can safely ferry excess cholesterol out of the body over the course of your lifetime, so much the better. Over time, cholesterol and fat deposits can block the passage of blood through the coronary arteries, possibly triggering a heart attack or stroke. That hardening of the arteries is called atherosclerosis.

New Hope for Kidney Patients

But for some people, lowering cholesterol is not just a long-term strategy. It is an immediate concern.

People with kidney disease, for example, are quite vulnerable to increased blood fat and an increase of atherosclerosis. In fact, atherosclerosis is one of the leading causes of death among long-term dialysis patients because of the abnormal lipid metabolism of failing kidneys.

Previous research by Dr. Friedman and his associates addressed the kidney patient's urgent concerns about atherosclerosis. Aware of charcoal's stick-to-itiveness, Dr. Friedman tried using charcoal to lower harmful blood fats.

"We were looking for a way to lower blood fat levels without hurting the person," recalls Dr. Friedman. "We knew that charcoal was cheaper and probably safer than drugs."

In Dr. Friedman's study, six patients took 35 grams of charcoal—a little over an ounce—every day. At the end of 24 weeks, cholesterol levels had dropped as much as 43 percent. Levels of triglycerides, another blood fat, fell as much as 76 percent.

Although the study didn't differentiate between LDL and HDL, the findings were significant, since overall cholesterol levels in many patients dropped, particularly among those with the highest cholesterol.

Cholesterol reduction is particularly important for those at immediate risk, such as kidney patients, but it's also a priority for the rest of us.

According to nationwide studies, more than half of all adult men have cholesterol levels high enough to put them at risk for heart attack. Dietary changes—such as reducing intake of saturated fat and cholesterol—will go a long way toward reducing that risk for those of us who don't yet have heart disease.

But according to the Finnish researchers, more needs to be done for people who already have dangerously high cholesterol levels. The results of their study of activated charcoal, they conclude, suggest this harmless and potentially helpful substance is an avenue of research clearly worth pursuing.

The American Heart Association's Guide to Healthy Eating

Heart disease used to be something that just "happened" to you. You could blame it on genes, getting older or just about any other handy excuse, but there wasn't a whole lot you could do about it. These days we know better. We know that smoking, inactivity and, especially, poor food choices may multiply our risk many times over.

Helping to prevent heart disease is what the American Heart Association (AHA) is all about. Since 1961, when the AHA delivered its first dietary guidelines to an overweight public, its goal has been to provide the practical advice people need to develop healthier eating habits.

The AHA has told American families how to cut back on cholesterol, salt, saturated fats, total fats and excess calories and how to fill up on whole grains, vegetables, fruits, low-fat dairy products, lean meats, fish and poultry.

The details follow, as AHA experts offer guidelines on how to shop for healthful foods, read a food label, trim fat and salt from your favorite recipes and other ways to eat well without doing yourself in.

New Guidelines for the Prudent

The American Heart Association recently revised its dietary guidelines to reflect the latest research findings on diet and heart disease. This updating refines and adds to earlier recommendations.

1. Total fat intake should be less than 30 percent of calories, down from a previous recommendation of 30 to 35 percent. Since most people still get about 40 percent of their calories from fat, this means that 10 percent of the calories you would normally eat as fat (200 to 270 calories) should be either cut out or replaced by other sources, such as carbohydrates.

2. Saturated fat should make up no more than 10 percent of your total calories. For most people this means cutting their saturated fat intake in half. (A man eating 2,700 calories a day should keep his saturated fat intake to 30 grams, the equivalent of about two tablespoons of pure saturated fat. For a woman eating 2,000 calories a day, that's 22 grams of fat or about 1½ tablespoons.)

   Most people can meet this requirement by cutting back on fatty red meat, butter, dairy fats and highly saturated vegetable fats such as coconut and palm oil, found in such processed foods as nondairy creamers and bakery goods.

   Of the remaining 20 percent of fat calories, less than half should come from polyunsaturates (such as safflower oil and corn oil) and the remainder should come from monounsaturates (such as olive oil).

3. Cholesterol intake should be less than 100 milligrams per 1,000 calories, not to exceed a total of 300 milligrams per day. Most people get that much cholesterol now in the meat, dairy and bakery products they eat. Since one egg has almost 300 milligrams of cholesterol, that means people

who want to stay within the guidelines will be limited to about two whole eggs a week.

4. Protein intake should be approximately 15 percent of calories. This does not significantly change total protein intake for the average American.

5. Carbohydrates should make up 50 percent or more of calories, with emphasis on increasing intake of complex carbohydrates such as whole grains, beans, vegetables and fruit. Right now most Americans get about 40 percent of their calories from carbohydrates—about one-third of which is from sugar.

6. Sodium intake should be reduced to approximately one gram per 1,000 calories, not to exceed three grams per day (that's 1½ level teaspoons of salt). This is far less than the six to eight grams a day the average American consumes. Not using salt in cooking or at the table and avoiding high-salt foods can help you cut sodium intake back to two grams.

7. Alcoholic beverages should be limited to no more than two beers or two glasses of wine a day. People who have more than three drinks a day experience a significant increase in blood pressure. And even moderate drinking can pile on the calories.

8. Total calories should be sufficient to maintain your best body weight.

9. A wide variety of foods should be eaten. Including many different kinds of foods in your diet helps assure that you get all the vitamins, minerals and other essential nutrients you need. Keeping your food selections varied and interesting also helps you stick with your new health-promoting diet.

The Heart-Healthy Kitchen

Complaints are rare in Gail Becker's kitchen, although creating tasty, healthy meals for a husband raised on heavy cream is a challenge even to this credentials-laden dietitian. In addition to her AHA activities, Becker is a cookbook author and president of a firm that helps major food companies market healthier products. She's also a wife concerned about her husband's potential for heart disease. Her tricks have literally filled books. Among them: Don't tell your family something is good for them until *after* they've eaten it. Disguise dishes so the healthy version tastes as good as the original. Avert total rebellion by changing gradually to lower-fat, lower-sodium and lower-calorie menus. And don't let an occasional ice cream parlor foray destroy your good humor — or your resolve to eat better.

Put Your Favorite Recipe on a Diet

Just about any recipe can be altered to meet AHA guidelines, Becker says. "You must realize, though, that you just can't cut back on the fat and salt. You need to replace fat with a liquid and the salt with other flavors."

Start by reducing the fat by 25 percent. The next time you make the dish, try cutting the fat by another 25 percent. Trim fat content as low as you can go and still enjoy the food.

There are many ways to cut fat (and salt) when preparing and cooking foods, without sacrificing flavor. Here are some examples.

- Use ground turkey (without skin) instead of ground beef in meat loaf or spaghetti sauce.
- Use less meat and more vegetables and grains in casseroles.
- Remember that for the same five grams of fat, you can eat either three ounces of skinless chicken, ten ounces of haddock or six cups of kidney beans.
- Make foods hot. Tex-Mex and Cajun cooking adapt well to low-fat, low-salt methods because the strong, spicy flavors need no help.
- Add wine, port or sherry to soups, stews and sauces. Cook for half an hour after adding to evaporate the alcohol but keep

the flavor. When making refried beans or bean soups, skip the lard and add beer for flavor, texture and moisture.

- Brush mustard on broiled fish or chicken. Add a little paprika, red pepper or parsley.
- Add pineapple, mandarin oranges or other fruits to chicken dishes. Brush orange juice concentrate on broiled fish or chicken. Instead of piling on the mayo, add mango, papaya, a few pine nuts and a little honey to chicken salad. A fruit salad dressing of pureed bananas, yogurt, poppyseed and orange juice contains only 30 calories a tablespoon.
- Use pureed potatoes, carrots, beans or French breads to thicken soups.

Using herbs instead of salt to season food can keep foods flavorful without driving up blood pressure in salt-sensitive people, thus controlling yet another risk factor for heart disease.

- Instead of butter and milk, use cinnamon and fruit butters or Butter Buds (fat-free, butter-flavored powder) on hot cereals.
- Add texture and taste to foods with sesame seeds, sunflower seeds or water chestnuts.
- When using yogurt in a heated sauce, first whisk two teaspoons of flour into each cup of yogurt to keep it from separating.
- Start a windowsill garden of your favorite herbs. Then experiment with gourmet delights like pungent baked rosemary chicken, parsley-walnut pesto or poached salmon with dill and yogurt sauce.
- Always use a nonstick pan or spray. "It's true that foods taste flat without the flavor of butter or margarine," Becker says. "So I sprinkle Butter Buds on scrambled eggs, vegetables and

Deciphering Food Labels

You can pick the healthiest frozen, canned and packaged foods once you learn a few simple things about labels. Let's say you're looking at the label on a package of low-calorie zucchini lasagna.

First, see how many calories are in one serving. In this case, the label says there are 260 calories.

Second, find the number of grams of fat per serving. The label says there are seven grams of fat per serving in this product.

Next, find the percentage of calories from fat. To do this, multiply the number of grams of fat per serving by nine (the number of calories per one gram of fat). Then divide by the total number of calories. The lasagna comes out to 24 percent of calories from fat ($7 \times 9 = 63 \div 260 = 0.24$ or 24 percent).

Most frozen dinners are about 300 calories, so if they have ten grams or less of fat, less than 30 percent of their calories are from fat.

rice." If you want to sauté vegetables, try using a little water or low-sodium broth instead of oil.

- Trim and discard any visible fat on meats before and after the meat is cooked. Remove chicken skin before cooking.
- Serve smaller portions of meat. Make meat a part of a larger dish like a stir-fry, stew or bean-packed chili. Cut the meat sukiyaki style—in thin strips on a diagonal—for the illusion of a larger serving.
- Before making stew or soup, chill the broth. The excess fat will rise to the top and harden, so you can easily skim it off.
- Always buy lower-fat versions of meats, cheeses, milk and other foods when available. And remember that, in enough quantity, even low-fat foods pile on the pounds.
- In cakes, pudding and pies, add extracts (coconut, almond,

Now find the amount of sodium per serving. That's 975 milligrams in this case. (To meet AHA guidelines, you should aim for no more than 1,000 milligrams of sodium for every 1,000 calories in your diet. Many frozen prepared foods have much more.)

If salt is not listed per serving, check the ingredients panel to see how many times sodium is mentioned, either as salt or as a form of sodium, like monosodium glutamate. If salt or any other ingredient that contains sodium is among the first five ingredients, play it safe and assume the product is high in sodium. And remember, the more often salt or any other sodium-containing ingredient appears, the higher the sodium content. (Ingredients are listed in descending order by weight. That means that the higher up on the list a sodium-containing ingredient is found, the more sodium there is in the product.)

Finally, compare several different brands of the same product. Choose one that has acceptable levels of both fat and salt.

vanilla, rum or even butter) to boost flavor while you cut back
on salt, fat and sugar.

- Substitute the same amount of low-fat yogurt or buttermilk
  for sour cream, milk or butter in baked goods.
- Help retain moisture in muffins and pancakes by adding
  moistened oatmeal or bran.
- When baking, use egg whites with a little added vegetable oil
  and nonfat dry milk powder in place of whole eggs.
- For flavor in baked goods, use a small amount of walnut or
  sesame oil or Butter Buds.

A Course in Supermarket Savvy

"People learn best from hands-on experience," says Dallas dietitian and author Leni Reed Reily.

That's why this AHA volunteer conducts her Supermarket Savvy
Tour in a well-stocked grocery store. The tour is an aisle-by-aisle course
in reading labels, interpreting advertising claims and learning which
foods contain reasonably low amounts of fat, salt, cholesterol and
calories.

Many who sign up for Riley's class do so at their doctor's behest.
They need to change their eating habits to lose weight, control their
blood pressure or reduce their risk of heart disease.

These people often don't have the time to cook from scratch, so
they need to know which are their best supermarket choices, especially
among the convenience foods.

"My goal is to show them that there are ways to cut corners and
time and still eat very nutritiously," says Riley, who is president of a
supermarket consulting firm.

Here are some of her suggestions.

- Choose among these bread products: For *little to no fat,* pick
  pita bread (preferably whole grain), rice cakes or unfried corn
  tortillas. For *low fat,* buy whole grain or partially whole grain
  breads, sandwich buns or English muffins. Other low-fat
  breads include Italian, French and water bagels (not
  egg bagels).
- For low-fat pancakes and waffles, choose whole wheat or

partially whole wheat mixes. Then, according to directions, add a polyunsaturated oil and substitute two egg whites for each whole egg. Cook on a nonstick skillet or waffle iron greased with just a little bit of an acceptable oil.

- Choose cooked cereals that you can make without salt (grits, mixed grain, oatmeal, rice and wheat) or cold cereals such as puffed rice, puffed wheat or shredded wheat. Avoid instant cooked cereals, because they generally contain sodium. Note that granola cereals often have at least twice as many calories as most other cereals. Avoid those granolas made with coconut oil, palm oil or vegetable shortening—the catchall term for vegetable oils, be they polyunsaturated like soybean and corn *or* saturated like coconut and palm.

- Make a can of low-sodium broth (beef or chicken) into a quick, healthy meal by adding fresh or frozen vegetables, cooked chicken chunks or diced tofu, fresh or dried herbs, and a little sherry, freshly grated ginger and/or hot-pepper sauce.

- Delicatessen items, usually high in fat and salt, can still be adapted to a healthy menu. With chicken or tuna salad, for instance, add more vegetables and pasta or rice to dilute the mayonnaise.

- Check out Worcestershire sauce, now available in a white-wine flavor. "Worcestershire sauce has only 55 milligrams of sodium per tablespoon, while regular soy sauce has 1,000 milligrams," Riley says. "And you get a lot of flavor out of just a tablespoon."

- When you see labels that say "lower" or "reduced" fat, salt or sugar, "you should ask 'lower than or reduced from *what?*' " Riley says. A package of chicken franks, for instance, says "lower fat," but the label shows that 72 out of the 90 calories in one frank are from fat. "Since that's lower fat, you can imagine what regular is like. Sliced boneless breast of turkey or lean ham would be a much better choice.

  "You can rinse much of the salt and sodium nitrite off the ham with cold water," she says. But be sure to use the ham immediately, because the salt and sodium nitrite act as preservatives.

- Don't assume that all-beef hot dogs are made from lean beef. All-beef hot dogs actually contain just as much fat as regular hot dogs; the fat in hot dogs is beef fat, not pork fat.
- Most frozen yogurt desserts are much lower in fat than frozen tofu desserts, which may contain corn, palm or coconut oil. But don't expect frozen yogurt to be much lower in calories than most ice creams. What they lack in fat, they make up in sugar. The new fruit sorbets are a delicious, low-calorie alternative to ice cream.
- Look for no-salt or lightly salted peanut butters without hydrogenated oils added to them.

For additional information on healthy eating, cooking and shopping, contact your local American Heart Association. For heart-healthy recipes and menu plans, see *The American Heart Association Cookbook,* available in most bookstores.

Does Your Meat Make the Grade?

Fancier cuts of meat are your worst choices when it comes to heart health. That's because the more fat in a meat, the better "grade" it currently gets. This discriminates against lean beef by giving the best-sounding, highest grades, such as "prime" and "choice" to the fattiest, not the healthiest, cuts.

For lean beef cuts, buy flank steak, round steak or sirloin steak, round roast—top, bottom or eye of round—rump roast or sirloin tip. Or choose extra-lean ground round. In pork, pick loin chops (also called center-cut pork chops), or fresh ham (pork leg) and Canadian bacon or lean boiled center-slice ham. (Rinse Canadian bacon and ham in water to remove some salt.)

CHAPTER
SEVEN

Reshape Your Body and Recharge Your Heart

By Kenneth Cooper, M.D.

Recently a young friend of mine was telling me about his life and career. At age 30, he was beginning to enjoy some of the sweet financial fruits of his years of labor in the corporate world. Times were good, and the future looked better.

I applauded his achievements and his investment savvy. But when I asked him what kind of investment he was making in his personal fitness and well-being, he said he really hadn't thought much about it. No, he didn't have a regular workout routine; he was too busy. But he did play softball once a week on the company team. "Doesn't that count?" he asked.

Besides, he said, he was still young. Sure, there was stress on the job, but it was bearable. Maybe in a few more years, when he had established himself a little more in the company, he would be in a position to take time to exercise. But for the moment, he was on the fast track, and a commitment to fitness was out of the question.

I told him that total fitness was not a luxury item but was one of the most important investments he could make, because it wouldn't do

43

any good for him to work so hard to make his dreams come true if he wasn't around to enjoy them.

My friend is not alone. There are millions of people in this country who are in exactly the same position. They have reached the age and position where good things are beginning to happen in their lives, but too many of them are failing to invest in life, failing to achieve the kind of quality life-style that fitness can provide.

It doesn't take long for dividends of a fitness life-style to pile up. They include:

- More personal energy and stamina.
- More enjoyable and active leisure time.
- Greater ability to handle domestic and job-related stress.
- Less depression, less hypochondria, less anxiety.
- Fewer physical complaints.
- Better self-image and more self-confidence.
- More restful sleep.
- Stronger bones.
- A more attractive, streamlined body.
- Better concentration.

An investment in total fitness can lower your risk of heart disease and pay other health dividends as well.

- Greater productivity.
- Lower risk of heart disease

Exercise, of course, is no cure-all, and it takes more than just sweat to earn the dividends of complete wellness. (Other important factors are weight control, diet, avoidance of tobacco, elimination or control of alcohol and habit-forming drugs, stress management and periodic physical examinations.) But there's no question that a program of exercise can be a key element in improving the quality of your life and helping you protect that most important investment of all—yourself.

Taking Stock

One of your major goals in life should be to achieve the balance of body and emotions that results in total well-being. But without a regular physical exam to determine that state of balance, there's no way to know exactly where you stand. After all, in most cases the starting line for a fitness program is in the doctor's office. The long view is that a regular physical may make it unnecessary for your physician to say, "I wish you'd come to me sooner."

The annual physical has gone the way of the Model T, but the less frequent medical checkup is alive and well—and essential for those in search of the good life of health and fitness. From ages 30 to 35, you should have a thorough exam every two years. I believe that a baseline physical exam at age 35 is extremely important for future reference. If the results of the age-35 checkup are normal, your next exam should be done at age 40, then every three years thereafter. (Ideally, after age 40, exams should be done at 18-month intervals, and past 50, at yearly intervals. But this ideal schedule is not always practical because of cost and availability.)

The physical exam should include a resting electrocardiogram, stress electrocardiogram (stress test), mammography for women, assessment of body fat, complete blood chemistry and, by age 40, an examination of the upper and lower colon.

The stress test, a special way of monitoring your heart while you're walking on a treadmill, is probably the most crucial assessment of your cardiovascular fitness. It can provide a basis for recommending the type and amount of exercise you should be doing. And, more important, it can detect the early stages of heart disease.

By administering the test to tens of thousands of people at our Aerobics Center, we found that the most reliable predictor of future heart attacks was the amount of time patients were able to walk on the treadmill—the longer they could go before exhaustion, the lower their risk of heart attack. We were also able to establish a minimum fitness standard for middle-aged people: They should be able to walk at least 15 minutes on the treadmill, roughly equivalent to running two miles in 20 minutes. Above this level of fitness, there seems to be some protection from heart disease. Below this level is risky territory.

Pumping Oxygen

Despite the upsurge of interest in fitness and the popularity of a well-toned body, most people are sedentary. They've therefore placed a low ceiling on their potential for achievement and well-being and—worst of all—put themselves at greater risk for heart disease.

But aerobic exercise—the kind that improves your body's use of oxygen—reverses these dangerous trends. Besides making you feel and look better, it boosts your lung capacity, strengthens your heart muscle, increases your blood level of high-density lipoprotein (HDL) cholesterol, which is the beneficial type, and promotes less clotting in the blood—all of which are associated with either greater longevity or less heart disease.

Aerobic exercise usually involves relatively slow, rhythmic movements of the legs or arms, as in jogging, cycling, rowing and stair climbing. But, more important, it also entails a sustained, elevated heart rate. If you keep your heart rate high enough long enough during an aerobic workout, you get what is known as a "training effect," another name for the beneficial changes in your cardiovascular system.

How hard must you exercise to reap these benefits? One valid answer is that you have to work up to your "target heart rate" and maintain it for 20 minutes four times a week, or 30 minutes three times a week. (If you're a man, you calculate your target heart rate by first subtracting half your age from 205; if you're a woman, you subtract your age from 220. The result is your predicted maximum heart rate. Take 80 percent of that, and you have your target heart rate.)

Another answer is that you can achieve a minimum training effect (and automatically boost your heart rate to an appropriate level) by chalking up a certain number of "aerobic points" each week.

I developed the aerobic points system to help people gauge the aerobic value (energy output) of different aerobic workouts. The greater the value, the more points assigned to a given workout. Obviously, the aerobic value (and thus the health value) of a workout has to depend on the kind of exercise you do, how many times a week you do it and how high you push your heart rate. The aerobic point system takes all this into account and makes it easy to compare one kind of aerobic workout with another and to keep track of how much aerobic benefit you're getting.

Through research at the Aerobics Center we've been able to accurately assign point values to many different kinds of exercise done at different intensities (measured by heart rate) and for different lengths of time. (See the tables on pages 50 through 55.) We've also determined the minimum number of aerobic points needed to get a good training effect—about 35 points per week for men, 30 points for women. Exercising below this level will, of course, earn you some physical benefit but not much cardiovascular advantage. Above the minimum level are the higher plains of fitness—50 to 55 points per week to attain excellent fitness, 70 to 80 points per week to reach the superior category.

The nice thing about the point system is that it gives you flexibility in your exercise program. For example, if you're 49 years old and you want to chalk up at least 30 points a week, you could walk 2½ miles in 37 minutes five times a week, or cycle 6 miles in 24 minutes four times a week, or run 2 miles in less than 20 minutes four times a week, or try some self-styled combination of aerobic exercises. Your workouts could be slow or fast, hard or soft, and still meet your weekly point quota.

The road to fitness, however, has speed limits and caution lights. If, for instance, you try to cram 30 aerobic points into two workouts per week, you risk sprains, strains or worse. And if you're over 40 years old and try to do a week's worth of exercise in one workout, you're begging for catastrophe. For safety's sake—and to maintain your level of aerobic conditioning—you should spread out your workouts to at least three different days.

It isn't necessary, though, to work your body more than five days a week. And seven days a week? Forget it. If you push yourself to maximum performance every day, you'll almost certainly suffer from cumulative fatigue and risk muscle, joint and bone injuries. Even on a five-day schedule I recommend alternating hard and easy days. After a certain point—probably above 85 points per week—vigorous exercise adds little to your cardiovascular health.

You also have to build safety into the workout itself. This requires a warm-up phase before you do your aerobics, a cool-down phase afterward, and some supplemental calisthenics or weight training several times a week. These are crucial for everyone but absolutely mandatory for people over 35.

The warm-up phase is two to three minutes of slow stretching to gradually speed up your heart rate before starting your aerobic workout and warm up your muscles so you can avoid injuries. The cool-down phase is at least five minutes of slowly walking about (no standing allowed!) after your regular workout. It gives your heart a chance to pump blood from your legs back into the central circulatory system— and thus protects you from dizziness, light-headedness or worse. The weight training or calisthenics (such as push-ups and sit-ups) helps protect you from injury during aerobic exercise by strengthening and toughening your muscles.

When you choose an aerobic exercise, you have to find a good match for your mind as well as your muscles. A cardinal rule of selection is: Choose a workout because you like it, not just because it's good for you. If you don't like to run, don't. Try fast walking. Hate racquetball? Try swimming. If you hate an exercise, you won't stick with it.

Another rule of selection: Consider any musculoskeletal problems you might have. If you have chronic knee or ankle problems, for example, forgo jogging or aerobic dance. Instead, try walking, stationary cycling or swimming.

And if weight loss is a big concern, you should think about an exercise's potential for burning calories. Diet should be your primary method of slimming down, but exercise can be an important adjunct to your efforts. Though a single workout doesn't consume a tremendous number of calories, regular workouts can knock off a pound of fat (equal to 3,500 calories) every two to three weeks—assuming, of course, that your calorie intake doesn't increase.

The Pace of Fitness:
Your Week-to-Week Workout Plan

The information in the tables on the following pages should help you assess these and other factors for some of America's most popular aerobic activities. The tables also show you how to ease into aerobic workouts, letting you earn enough aerobic points without breaking your body's speed limit.

They're fitness schedules customized especially for people 30 years old and older. By the time you reach the last week on most of the charts (week 7 or 8 on the jogging charts), you will have achieved a respectable minimum of aerobic conditioning. You can maintain that level indefinitely, slowly push on toward more aerobic points per week or try other aerobic exercises. Just remember that the time goals listed are to be reached at the end of each week, not at the beginning. And if you have trouble with the requirements of a week, repeat it until you master them.

Swimming

Potential for injury: Low.

Calories burned per hour: 530 (crawl, 45 yards per minute).

Age restrictions: None.

Comments: Swimming involves all the major muscles in the body and thus gives you more of an all-around conditioning than many other sports. Swimmers tend to have fewer injuries than runners because the buoyancy of the water helps reduce excessive pressure on the joints and bones. Swimming is an excellent exercise for people with arthritis.

Ages 30 to 49

Week	1	2	3	4	5	6	7	8	9	10
Times/wk.	4	4	4	4	4	4	4	4	4	4
Distance (yd.)	300	300	400	400	500	500	600	700	800	900
Time goal (min.)	12	10	13	12	14	13	16	19	22	22:30
Aerobic points	6.2	7.5	10.2	11.1	14.9	16.0	18.8	23.5	28.2	36.0

Ages 50 and older

Week	1	2	3	4	5	6	7	8	9	10	11	12
Times/wk.	4	4	4	4	4	4	4	4	4	4	4	4
Distance (yd.)	300	300	400	400	500	500	600	600	700	700	800	800
Time goal (min.)	15	12	15	13	16	14	17	15	20	18	22	20
Aerobic points	5.0	6.2	8.9	10.2	13.0	14.9	17.6	20.0	22.4	24.7	28.2	30.7

Outdoor Cycling

Potential for injury: Low.

Calories burned per hour: 540 to 600 (13 mph).

Age restrictions: Not recommended for people 65 years old and older who don't cycle regularly, but fine for those who have been cyclists previously. To avoid falls, three-wheeled cycling is best for the older age group.

Comments: This exercise is far easier on joints and muscles than jogging, so people with joint and knee problems may prefer it. Generally, speeds less than 10 miles per hour are worth very little aerobically. For most people, cycling speeds slightly greater than 15 miles per hour are optimum for a training effect.

Ages 30 to 49

Week	1	2	3	4	5	6	7	8	9	10
Times/wk.	3	3	4	4	4	4	4	4	4	4
Distance (mi.)	4	4	5	5	5	6	6	7	7	7
Time goal (min.)	20	18	24	22	20	26	24	30	26	27
Aerobic points	10.0	11.5	19.0	21.3	24.0	27.2	30.0	33.2	36.0	36.1

Ages 50 and older

Week	1	2	3	4	5	6	7	8	9	10	11	12
Times/wk.	3	3	4	4	4	4	4	4	4	4	4	4
Distance (mi.)	3	3	4	4	5	5	5	6	6	7	7	7
Time goal (min.)	20	18	26	24	32	28	24	30	26	32	30	28
Aerobic points	3.6	4.5	9.4	10.0	12.8	15.4	19.0	22.8	27.2	30.8	33.2	36.0

Jogging

Potential for injury: Moderate.

Calories burned per hour: 650 (5.5 mph).

Age restrictions: Not recommended for inactive people 60 years old and older, but fine for those 60 and over who have been running or jogging previously or are on a medically supervised progressive jogging program.

Comments: I draw a distinction between jogging and running. Jogging is going slower than nine minutes per mile; running is going faster than that. Most people who want aerobic conditioning choose jogging because it's so convenient (almost any street or sidewalk will do) and requires little skill compared to swimming or cross-country skiing. Most injuries occur when you fail to warm up or start running excessive distances—about 25 miles per week or more.

Week							Ages 30 to 49					
	1	2	3	4	5	6	7	8	9	10	11	12
Activity	Walk			Walk/Jog		Jog						
Times/wk.	3	3	3	4	4	4	4	4	4	4	4	4
Distance (mi.)	2	2.5	3	2	2	2	2.5	2.5	2.5	3		3
Time goal (min.)	34	42	50	25	24	22	20	26	25	31	29	27
Aerobic points	12.2	16.3	20.4	26.4	28.0	31.6	36.0	43.7	46.0	53.7	57.6	61.3

Ages 50 and older

Week	1	2	3	4	5	6	7	8	9	10	11	12
Activity	Walk				Walk/Jog		Jog					
Times/wk.	5	4	3	4	4	4	4	4	4	4	4	4
Distance (mi.)	1	2	3	3	2	2	2	2	2.5	2.5	3	3
Time goal (min.)	18	36	54	52	26	24	22	20	27	25	32	30
Aerobic points	5.3	14.7	18.0	25.6	24.9	28.0	31.6	36.0	41.6	46.0	51.5	56.0

Walking

Potential for injury: Very low.

Calories burned per hour: 400 (4.5 mph).

Age restrictions: None.

Comments: Walking is one of the world's best exercises. In fact, it can be every bit as good for you as running is. Studies have shown that if you walk 12 minutes per mile, you can expend more energy than if you run at the same speed — 96 calories per mile for running, 106 for walking. The reason is that running is nature's overdrive: At higher speeds, it's more efficient than walking. So if you walk fast and resist the urge to slip into overdrive, you can actually burn up more calories than when you run. But even at paces less than 12 minutes per mile, walking is still an excellent aerobic exercise with a minimal potential for injury and high potential for enjoyment.

Ages 30 to 49

Week	1	2	3	4	5	6	7	8	9	10
Times/wk.	3	3	4	4	4	5	5	5	5	4
Distance (mi.)	2	2	2	2	2.5	2.5	2.5	3	3	3
Time goal (min.)	36	34	32	30	39	38	37	46	45	44
Aerobic points	11.0	12.2	18.0	20.0	24.5	31.8	33.2	38.7	40.0	33.1

Ages 50 and older

Week	1	2	3	4	5	6	7	8	9	10	11	12
Times/wk.	4	4	4	4	4	4	4	4	4	4	4	4
Distance (mi.)	1	1.5	2	2	2	2	2.5	2.5	2.5	3	3	3
Time goal (min.)	20	30	40	38	36	34	42	40	38	47	46	45
Aerobic points	4.0	8.0	12.0	13.3	14.7	16.2	21.7	23.5	25.5	30.0	31.0	32.0

Recipes for Lower Cholesterol

Throughout this book, we have been emphasizing the effect that diet can have on lowering cholesterol. In this chapter we offer some recipes for appetizing, satisfying dishes that will help you make the change to a more healthful diet—deliciously.

Tasty High-Fiber Breakfasts

Is your usual breakfast a lavish production complete with fresh flowers and the newspaper? Or is it more like a brown-bag affair for eating a la commute? Either way, a menu featuring fiber-rich foods can benefit your body long after the morning's gone.

From the simple prune to hot, fruity cereals, high-fiber breakfasts may help fend off disease, including heart disease.

Raisin and Sweet Potato Scones

½ cup unbleached flour
½ cup whole wheat flour
½ cup corn bran
½ cup raisins, chopped
½ cup shredded sweet
   potato
1 teaspoon cream of
   tartar
½ teaspoon baking soda

pinch of ground
   cinnamon
pinch of grated
   nutmeg
⅓ cup plus 1 tablespoon
   buttermilk
2 tablespoons oil

In a large bowl, mix flours, bran, raisins, sweet potato, cream of tartar, baking soda, cinnamon and nutmeg. Stir in buttermilk and oil until blended. With floured hands, knead mixture for about 2 minutes.

Preheat oven to 475°F.

On a lightly floured surface, roll out dough ¼ inch thick. Cut out 2½-inch rounds, transferring each to a lightly oiled cookie sheet as you go. Use all dough by rerolling leftovers. Bake for 6 to 8 minutes. Serve warm.

Yield: 18; about 3 grams of dietary fiber per scone

Eggs Diablo

Broccoli and whole wheat muffins perk up the fiber content of eggs.

⅓	cup low-fat yogurt	8	thin broccoli stalks, steamed
1	teaspoon Dijon mustard	4	poached eggs
½	teaspoon dried tarragon		minced fresh parsley (garnish)
2	whole wheat English muffins, split and toasted		

In a small bowl, combine yogurt, mustard and tarragon.
Place muffins on individual plates. Top with broccoli and eggs. Spoon on yogurt sauce and sprinkle with parsley.

Yield: 4 servings; about 4 grams of dietary fiber per serving

Raspberry Bread Pudding

The wheat germ, bran, whole wheat bread and raspberries all contribute fiber. Serve with vanilla yogurt.

4	slices whole wheat bread	2	eggs or ½ cup egg substitute
⅓	cup wheat germ	2	tablespoons maple syrup
2	tablespoons bran	1	teaspoon vanilla extract
2	cups raspberries		
1	cup orange juice		
1	cup skim milk		

Coat a 1½-quart ovenproof casserole with nonstick spray.

Tear bread into small pieces. Place in casserole with wheat germ, bran and raspberries. Toss to combine.

Preheat oven to 375°F.

In a medium bowl, whisk together juice, milk, eggs, syrup and vanilla. Pour over bread mixture and press bread into liquid. Bake for 40 to 45 minutes, or until all liquid has been absorbed.

Yield: 6 servings; about 4 grams of dietary fiber per serving

Spanish Omelet

Adding potatoes to an omelet increases fiber content.

2	small potatoes, diced	1	tablespoon minced
1	onion, minced		fresh parsley
1	tomato, peeled,	4	eggs, lightly beaten,
	seeded and diced		or 1 cup egg
2	cloves garlic, minced		substitute

In a large nonstick skillet, cook potatoes, onions, tomatoes, garlic and parsley in olive oil until potatoes are soft and most of the liquid has evaporated from tomatoes.

Add eggs. Cook over medium heat about 30 seconds, lifting cooked edges so that uncooked egg can run underneath. Turn heat to low, cover and cook until top is set.

Place a large plate upside-down on top of pan. Using pot holders, invert pan and turn omelet onto plate. Then slide omelet back into skillet, browned side up, and cook another 2 minutes. Cut into wedges to serve.

Yield: 2 servings; about 2.8 grams of dietary fiber per serving

Spanish Omelet

Kiwi and Pineapple Eye-Opener

Juices tend to be low in fiber because the fiber has been strained out.
Blending in whole fruit is a way to put a little back.

3	kiwifruit	strawberries
4	cups pineapple juice	(garnish)

Peel the kiwis and cut into small pieces. Place in a blender or
food processor and add pineapple juice. Process just until smooth.
Garnish with strawberries and serve as is or over crushed ice.

*Yield: 4 servings; about 1.8 grams of dietary fiber per
serving*

Banana Splits with Apricot Cream

Here's an unusual way to get both protein and fiber in a light breakfast.

1 pound low-fat cottage cheese	1 cup blueberries toasted wheat germ or sliced toasted almonds (garnish)
3 tablespoons apricot jam	
4 bananas	
1 cup sliced strawberries	

Spoon cottage cheese into a food processor or blender and process until completely smooth, scraping sides of container as necessary. Add jam and blend to combine. Transfer to a medium bowl, cover and refrigerate overnight.

Peel bananas, split each lengthwise and place two slices on each plate. Spoon some apricot cream over slices and top with strawberries and blueberries. Sprinkle with wheat germ or almonds.

Yield: 4 servings; about 3.8 grams of dietary fiber per serving

Prune Butter

Prunes, which are fiber champs, make a delicious spread. Serve with muffins, scones, pancakes or waffles. Prune butter also makes an excellent dip for apple slices.

2	cups (12 ounces) pitted prunes	1	vanilla bean pinch of grated orange peel
1¾	cups apple juice		
¼	cup raisins or 4 dried figs, stems removed		

In a 2-quart saucepan, combine prunes, juice, raisins or figs, vanilla bean and orange peel. Bring to a simmer and cook over low heat, stirring frequently, for 30 minutes.

Let mixture cool slightly. Remove and discard vanilla bean. Transfer mixture to a food processor or blender and process until smooth. (If mixture becomes too thick, thin with additional apple juice.)

Yield: about 2 cups; about 1.5 grams of dietary fiber per tablespoon

Fruit Compote

Make this ahead of time and serve warm or cold.

1	cup applesauce	¼	teaspoon grated nutmeg
1	cup apple juice		
	juice and grated rind of 1 lemon	½	cup dried apricot halves
1	tablespoon vanilla extract	¼	cup pitted prunes
		6	dried figs, halved
½	teaspoon ground cinnamon	¼	cup dried currants
¼	teaspoon powdered ginger	1	pear, thinly sliced

Preheat oven to 300°F.

In a 2-quart ovenproof casserole, combine applesauce, juice, lemon juice and rind, vanilla, cinnamon, ginger and nutmeg. Stir in apricots, prunes, figs, currants and pears. Cover and bake for 1½ hours.

Yield: 4 servings; about 5.4 grams of dietary fiber per serving

Apples and Oats

You get a double boost of fiber from this delicious cereal. Besides the fiber found in apples, oat bran contains water-soluble fiber, which scientists believe can help lower cholesterol and other blood fats in the body.

4 cups water	½ teaspoon ground
1⅓ cups oat bran	caraway (optional)
½ cup raisins or	½ teaspoon ground
currants	cinnamon
1 apple, shredded	
1 tablespoon maple	
syrup	

In a 2-quart saucepan, bring water and oat bran to a vigorous boil, stirring constantly. Reduce heat to low and cook for 2 minutes, stirring frequently, until thick.

Remove from heat and stir in raisins or currants, apples, syrup, caraway, if used, and cinnamon. Let stand 5 minutes before serving. Serve with skim milk.

Yield: 4 servings; about 10 grams of dietary fiber per serving

Note: You may cook this cereal ahead and reheat it in the microwave. Cover 1½ cups of cereal with plastic wrap, then microwave on high for about 2 minutes.

Quick Fiber
Breakfasts

When you're pressed for time in the morning, you can still have a tasty meal of cereal, breads and/or fruit that will boost your total fiber intake. Her are some quick suggestions that are a snap to put together.

- Spread rye crispbread with a thin layer of strawberry jam.
- Toss a handful of cooked corn kernels into hot cereal.
- Brush half a grapefruit with a little raspberry jam, then broil. Serve with whole grain bread.
- Fill a taco shell with sliced strawberries. Serve with vanilla yogurt.
- Create the perfect no-fat-added waffle. Bake a piece of whole grain bread in an ungreased waffle iron for 5 minutes, or until crisp and brown. Top with prune butter and vanilla yogurt.

Or you can take a few minutes the night before and make a refreshing fruit cup of cut-up strawberries, bananas, kiwifruit, raspberries, and apricots. Or bag up a bran muffin and a pear to eat on the way to work or school or when you get to your desk.

Check the table at right for some more good sources of fiber in quick-and-easy breakfast foods.

High-Fiber
Breakfast Foods

Food	Portion	Dietary Fiber (g.)
Cereals and Breads		
100% bran cereal	½ cup	8.4
Oat bran, uncooked	1 cup	7.8
Corn bran	2 tbsp.	6.6
40% bran flakes cereal	¾ cup	4.0
Wheat germ	¼ cup	3.4
Oatmeal, uncooked	½ cup	3.1
Wheat bran	2 tbsp.	2.7
Bran muffin	1	2.5
Whole wheat bread	1 slice	1.7
Fruit		
Raspberries	1 cup	5.8
Raisins	½ cup	4.9
Pear	1 med.	4.5
Prunes	5	4.0
Apple, with skin	1 med.	2.8
Banana	1 med.	2.7
Apricots	3	2.0
Kiwifruit	1	1.8
Strawberries	½ cup	1.6

Low-Calorie Soups

Hearty hot soups harken back to our childhood, when a brimming bowl of homemade goodness warmed us. Thick soups can still do that. Providing you steer away from heavy, cream-based varieties, luscious soups *can* fill you up without filling you out. Studies have even shown soup to play a valuable role as an appetite suppressant. And if served with a thick slice of unbuttered bread and a lightly dressed salad, soup can be a meal unto itself.

One good way to keep down the calories is to make your own stock. Prepare a large potful on a Sunday afternoon. Simmer it slowly until the flavor is meaty and rich. Strain, then refrigerate overnight. All the fat will rise to the top and solidify so you can easily skim it off. Set aside enough stock for a day or two's worth of soup, and freeze the rest in pint containers.

For the best flavor and optimum nutrition when making both soup and stock, don't peel vegetables such as carrots, potatoes, turnips and parsnips. Valuable nutrients lurk just under the skin.

Add body to soups with filling but low-fat ingredients such as dried beans, split peas, lentils, diced potatoes and tiny pasta. Remember that a little goes a long way. Bring out the flavor of vegetables with judicious use of dried herbs. You can even make cream-type soups by blending potatoes as thickening and adding skim milk.

Cuban Black Bean Soup

Popular in Latin America, this soup is a storehouse of nutrients and as satisfying a soup as you'll find. Ginger is a nontraditional addition.

¼	pound dried black beans	1	hot pepper, seeded and minced
1	medium onion, chopped	2	tablespoons minced parsley
1	tablespoon minced gingerroot	½	teaspoon dried thyme
2	cloves garlic, minced	1	bay leaf
1	stalk celery, thinly sliced	1	cup chicken stock
		2	teaspoons low-sodium soy sauce

In a large bowl, soak beans overnight in enough water to cover.

Preheat oven to 375°F.

Drain beans and place in a 2- or 3-quart ovenproof casserole. Add onions, ginger, garlic, celery, pepper, parsley, thyme and bay leaf. Add enough water to cover ingredients (about 2½ cups), then stir in stock and soy sauce.

Bake for 2 hours, or until beans are tender. Remove bay leaf before serving.

Yield: 4 servings; 118 calories per serving

Italian Escarole Soup

½	chicken breast, skin removed	1	cup sliced carrots
5	cups water	½	cup sliced parsnips
1	large carrot	½	cup chopped leeks
1	small onion	1½	cups chopped escarole
1	stalk celery		

Place chicken in a large saucepan with water, whole carrot, onion and celery. Bring to a boil, skim off any foam, then reduce heat, cover and simmer for 45 minutes. Remove chicken and set aside.

Continue to simmer stock for 30 minutes, then remove and discard the carrot, onion and celery.

When chicken is cool, remove meat from bones and cut into bite-sized chunks.

Add sliced carrots, parsnips and leeks to stock. Bring to a boil, then reduce heat and simmer until vegetables are tender, about 30 minutes. Add escarole and cook an additional 10 minutes. Add chicken and heat through before serving.

Yield: 5 servings; 54 calories per serving

Creamy Corn Chowder

2	tablespoons chicken stock	2	cups corn kernels
1	small sweet red pepper, finely diced	1¾	cups skim milk dash of grated nutmeg
3	scallions, minced	1	teaspoon low-sodium soy sauce
1	shallot, minced		
1	tablespoon whole wheat flour		

Place stock in a large saucepan over medium heat. Add peppers, scallions and shallots. Cook, stirring frequently, until peppers are crisp-tender, about 3 minutes. (If necessary, add a bit of water to prevent scorching.) Stir in flour and cook 1 to 2 minutes more, stirring constantly. Remove from heat.

Place 1 cup of corn in blender or food processor with 1 cup of milk. Process on low speed until smooth, scraping the sides of the container as necessary. Add blended mixture, remaining corn and milk, nutmeg and soy sauce to the pepper mixture in the saucepan. Place over medium heat and bring just to the boiling point, stirring frequently. Reduce heat and simmer for about 5 minutes before serving.

Yield: 4 servings; 123 calories per serving

Caspian Sea Split-Pea Soup

6	cups water	3	tablespoons minced parsley
2	large tomatoes, chopped	1	tablespoon low-sodium soy sauce
1	cup shredded cabbage	2	cloves garlic, minced
½	cup dried split peas		
½	cup barley		
2	large carrots, sliced diagonally		

Place 2 cups of water and the tomatoes in a blender or food processor. Process on low speed until smooth. Transfer to a large saucepan and add cabbage, split peas and barley.

Add remaining water and bring to a boil over medium-high heat. Add carrots, parsley, soy sauce and garlic.

Cover pan, reduce heat to simmer and cook for about 1¼ hours, or until barley is tender.

Yield: 6 servings; 148 calories per serving

Creamy Tomato Soup

1	potato, diced	¼	teaspoon pepper
2	carrots, diced	1½	cups beef stock
2	stalks celery, diced	1	16-ounce can
1	medium onion,		tomatoes
	chopped	2	tablespoons tomato
2	bay leaves		paste
1½	teaspoons dried basil	⅓	cup orzo or other tiny
¾	teaspoon dried		pasta, cooked
	oregano	1	cup low-fat yogurt
¼	teaspoon chili powder		

Place potatoes, carrots, celery, onions, bay leaves, basil, oregano, chili powder, pepper and stock in a large saucepan. Bring to a boil, then reduce heat, cover and simmer for 10 minutes, or until the vegetables are tender.

Stir in tomatoes and their juice. Add tomato paste and orzo or other pasta. Simmer 5 more minutes, or until heated through. Remove from heat and stir in yogurt. Remove bay leaves and serve immediately.

Yield: 4 servings; 164 calories per serving

Potato and Broccoli Vichyssoise

Serve this soup either warm or cold.

2	medium potatoes, chopped	¼	teaspoon dried thyme
1	to 1½ pounds broccoli, stalks only, sliced	⅛	teaspoon crushed rosemary
		⅛	teaspoon ground cumin
1	cup water	1	cup skim milk
1	large leek, sliced		

In a 3-quart saucepan, steam potatoes and broccoli over boiling water for 15 minutes, or until potatoes are tender. Set aside, reserving the cooking water.

In a small skillet, sauté leek in margarine or butter for several minutes, until limp. Add thyme, rosemary and cumin and cook for about 1 minute.

Place potatoes, broccoli, leek mixture, milk and ½ cup of cooking water in a blender or food processor and process until smooth. (If necessary, add a bit more cooking liquid to achieve desired consistency.)

Yield: 4 servings; 116 calories per serving

Eggplant Soup with Tiny Pasta

1	medium onion, minced	1¾	cups chicken stock
1	clove garlic, minced	⅛	teaspoon dried thyme
¼	cup minced celery leaf	⅛	teaspoon crushed rosemary
2	cups cubed eggplant	½	cup orzo or other tiny pasta, cooked
6	Italian plum tomatoes, peeled and chopped		

In a large saucepan, sauté onions, garlic and celery in olive oil for about 3 minutes. Add eggplant and tomatoes. Cover and simmer for about 10 minutes.

Add stock, thyme and rosemary and simmer for 20 minutes. Then add orzo or other pasta and heat through.

Yield: 4 servings; 137 calories per serving

Low-calorie soups: Clockwise from left are Italian Escarole Soup, Eggplant Soup with Tiny Pasta, Creamy Corn Chowder, Creamy Tomato Soup, Cuban Black Bean Soup, Potato and Broccoli Vichyssoise and Caspian Sea Split-Pea Soup (center).

Feasting on Healthy Appetizers

Have you noticed that people are eating differently than they used to? Oh, they still use knives and forks, but what's on their plates has changed. Gone are the big slabs of meat smothered in heavy sauce, and in their place is lighter fare, smaller portions, greater variety. The recent popularity of *tapas* restaurants, where diners enjoy a wide array of appetizers in lieu of a single large entrée, gives testament to a new style of eating.

If you'd like to savor lighter dishes that are both delicious and healthfully low in calories, we've got good news for you. There's a wide variety of foods to choose from that you can prepare with a minimum of fuss and a maximum of taste. Here are a few of our favorites to give you an idea of the possibilities.

Roasted sweet peppers.   Take your choice of red, green, yellow or black. On the average, a whole cooked pepper contains a mere 13 calories. Naturally, you can eat them raw. But for a change of pace, roast and peel them before serving.

To prepare roasted peppers, preheat your broiler. Place peppers on their sides in a pan and broil until their skins are blackened on all sides, about 20 minutes. Place the peppers in a paper bag, close the bag and let them stand until cool (this allows them to steam loose any bits of skin that weren't charred). Remove the core, inner membranes and charred skin. The peppers can then be cut into strips or minced for salads. Or puree them as a sauce for pasta or steamed vegetables.

Mushrooms.   With their "meaty" taste and aroma, mushrooms can satisfy a craving for meat, without all the fat and calories. A whole pound of fresh shiitake mushrooms, for example, contains only 181 calories, far less than a single burger. The common white mushrooms so widely available are even lower in calories.

For a taste treat, broil shiitake mushrooms. First remove their tough stems. Then marinate the caps in a light mixture of minced ginger, minced garlic and a small amount of soy sauce or Worcestershire sauce for about 15 minutes. Grill or broil for two or three minutes per side. Serve piping hot.

On the same theme, mix up a batch of *duxelles* to use as a stuffing for whole artichokes, fish fillets or steamed squash. *Duxelles* are nothing more than minced mushrooms that are cooked in a bit of stock with minced onions until the mixture is dark, fragrant and somewhat dry in the pan (meaning all the stock and mushroom liquid have cooked away). Season with a little tarragon, lemon juice and thyme. For variety, toss with steamed vegetables, chunks of steamed fish or steamed shrimp.

Unusual greens.   Add excitement to salads by sampling the gourmet greens that are available in the supermarkets and farmers' markets. They're all nicely low in calories and give any dish a special touch. As a bonus, many are easily grown from seed and would make a fine addition to your spring garden.

For taste appeal, try *mazuna,* a mustardy-tasting green that's great sautéed or raw. Sugar loaf chicory (*pain de sucre*), ruby lettuce and oak leaf lettuce can really make a salad interesting. So can old standbys that we often overlook today, such as dandelion and purslane.

Japanese noodles.   These are a welcome change from ordinary pasta. There is a wealth of varieties to choose from. Try *harusame,* also called spring rain, and *shiratake,* which are thin threads of vermicellilike noodles made from vegetable starch. These and many others are available at Oriental grocery stores and many large supermarkets.

The following recipes can be served individually as entrées or side dishes, but they're so festive and elegant that we hope you'll consider serving them as party food. Together they'll make a wonderful cocktail buffet that your guests will savor. And nobody will guess how nicely low in calories they are.

Braised Leeks with Mustard Sauce

1	pound leeks (preferably young, tender ones)	1	bay leaf
		1½	teaspoons Dijon mustard
1	cup chicken stock		minced fresh mint
¼	teaspoon mustard seed		

Slice off roots and tough green parts of leeks, then rinse leeks carefully to remove all sand and grit. If leeks are young and tender (less than 1 inch in diameter), leave them whole. Otherwise, cut each in half lengthwise, taking care not to disrupt the layers.

In a large skillet, combine stock, mustard seeds and bay leaf. Add leeks, cut side down. Bring to a simmer over medium heat, then cover and simmer for 8 minutes.

Remove lid and set pan in refrigerator for about 30 minutes to chill.

Remove leeks from pan and arrange on a serving platter. Strain and reserve stock.

Combine 3 tablespoons stock with mustard. Drizzle over leeks and sprinkle with mint.

Yield: 4 servings

Chilled Scallop Coins

¾	pound sea scallops	1	teaspoon cornstarch
2½	tablespoons chicken stock	1	tablespoon rice vinegar
½	teaspoon minced gingerroot		pinch of grated orange peel
2	cloves garlic, minced	1	yellow bell pepper, cut into slivers
½	pound snow peas		

Slice scallops in half crosswise, to make coin shapes.

In a large bowl, combine stock, ginger and garlic. Add scallops and toss to coat. Marinate for 15 minutes.

Prepare snow peas by removing strings and cutting pods into thirds on the diagonal. Set them in a colander and pour 1 quart of boiling water over them. Drain.

Drain scallops, reserving marinade.

Coat a large nonstick skillet with nonstick spray. Heat skillet and sauté scallops for 2 minutes. Add peas and toss to combine.

In a cup, combine reserved marinade with cornstarch. Pour over scallops. Cook over high heat, constantly tossing and turning the mixture, until sauce is shiny and thick. Transfer mixture to a large bowl, cover loosely and refrigerate until chilled.

Just before serving, add vinegar, orange peel and peppers. Combine well.

Yield: 4 servings

Chilled Scallop Coins

Japanese Noodles with Spinach Ribbons

2½	ounces thin rice-stick noodles	2	cloves garlic, minced
1½	cups chicken stock	8	ounces spinach leaves, sliced into thin ribbons
1½	teaspoons dried sage		
1	teaspoon low-sodium soy sauce	5	scallions, minced

Cook noodles in boiling water for 4 minutes. Drain and set aside.

In a large skillet, combine stock, sage, soy sauce and garlic. Bring to a simmer, then add noodles. Do not stir noodles or they will tangle; instead gently move them around, using chopsticks or tongs.

When noodles are heated, add spinach and scallions. Simmer about 20 seconds, or until spinach is wilted. Serve in shallow bowls.

Yield: 4 servings

Lean Sauces

There are lean times ahead. But the economy's not on the skids; it's the fat and calories in tasty sauces that are taking a dive. And it's about time.

Face it, sauces have always been a problem. True, nothing adds that special touch to meat, poultry, vegetables and fruit dishes like a smooth-as-silk sauce. But nothing spoils the sauce like a hefty load of fat. So how *do* you cut the fat without sacrificing flavor? By creating slim sauces from vegetable or fruit purees. It's that simple.

Start by cooking vegetables or fruit in stock, fruit juice or spicy herb tea. Add herbs, spices or other flavorings and puree until smooth. Serve as is, or simmer a bit to thicken the puree and enhance flavors. Even easier are sauces made by pureeing raw fruits or certain vegetables.

For versatility, turn your sauces into low-cal soups by whisking an appropriate amount of stock or skim milk into the puree.

To get you started enjoying lean sauces, here are some of our favorite flavor combinations.

- Serve a sauce made from cooked winter squash, apples, raisins and cinnamon with lean pork or roast turkey.
- A combination of cooked sweet potato, mashed banana and minced ginger goes well with poached chicken or lean pork.
- Cooked carrot, orange pulp, nutmeg and curry powder make a tasty sauce for roast chicken or cooked barley.
- Blueberries, orange rind and cinnamon are a combination that enhances fruit salad or frozen yogurt.
- Apricots, almond extract and vanilla extract make a yummy topping for bananas or pound cake.
- A sauce made from cooked pears, dried currants and white grapes can be served with citrus sections or fruit salad.

Savory Three-Root Sauce

Serve hot with lean roast meats, steamed broccoli or brussels sprouts.

2 large potatoes, peeled and chopped	3 parsnips, peeled and chopped
1 celery root (about 1 pound), peeled and chopped	2 cups chicken stock

Place potatoes in a medium saucepan and add cold water to cover. Bring to a boil and cook until tender, about 15 minutes. Drain and mash using a food mill, electric mixer or hand-held masher. (Do not use a food processor; potatoes will become gummy.)

In another medium saucepan, combine celery and parsnips. Add cold water to cover. Bring to a boil and cook until tender, about 15 minutes.

Place parsnips, celery and stock in a food processor or blender and process until smooth. Stir mixtures together and serve.

Yield: 6 cups

Santa Fe Sauce

Serve hot with poached fish, eggs, grilled chicken, lean pork, tortillas or zucchini and onions.

1	medium onion, chopped	½	teaspoon coriander seed, crushed
1	cup corn kernels	½	teaspoon dried oregano
3	cups peeled, seeded and chopped tomatoes	1	teaspoon chili powder
3	cloves garlic, minced	10	drops hot-pepper sauce
½	teaspoon cumin seed, crushed		

Place onions, corn, tomatoes and garlic in a food processor or blender and process until smooth. Pour into a medium saucepan, bring to a boil and cook uncovered for 7 minutes, stirring occasionally. Add cumin, coriander, oregano, chili powder and pepper sauce. Continue to boil, stirring often, for 8 to 10 minutes, or until sauce has reduced in volume by half.

Yield: about 2 cups

Red Pepper Coulis

Coulis is another name for a thick puree. Serve this sauce hot with poached fish, pasta or steamed asparagus or globe artichokes. Or serve cold with strips of thinly sliced beef or steamed shrimp.

5	sweet red peppers, coarsely chopped	2	cloves garlic, minced
½	cup stock	2	teaspoons dried basil
2	tablespoons balsamic vinegar		

Place ingredients in a food processor or blender and process until smooth. Pour into a medium saucepan and bring to a boil. Lower heat slightly and cook uncovered for 10 minutes, until sauce is thick and fragrant.

Yield: about 2 cups

Sweet Peach Sauce

Serve cold as a dressing for fruit salads or as a topping for cakes, crepes or poached fruit. If you're using fresh peaches, you'll need to cook the sauce a bit to thicken it.

1½	cups peeled, pitted and chopped fresh or frozen peaches (about 4)	2	teaspoons apple juice concentrate dash of freshly grated nutmeg

Place ingredients in a food processor or blender and process until smooth.

Yield: about 1 cup

Savory Peach Sauce

Serve cold with cold poached seafood. Or heat gently and serve with lean pork. If you're using fresh peaches, you'll need to cook the sauce a bit to thicken it.

1½	cups peeled, pitted and chopped fresh or frozen peaches (about 4)	1½	teaspoons prepared horseradish
2	teaspoons honey	1	teaspoon raspberry vinegar

Place ingredients in a food processor or blender and process until smooth.

Yield: about 1 cup

Luscious lean sauces: Clockwise from left are Red Pepper Coulis, Savory Three-Root Sauce, Peach Sauce and Blueberry-Orange Sauce.